D1514993

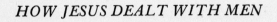

HOW JESUS DEALT WITH MEN

HOW JESUS
DEALT WITH MEN

By

RAYMOND CALKINS

ABINGDON-COKESBURY PRESS

New York ● *Nashville*

HOW JESUS DEALT WITH MEN

SET UP, PRINTED, AND BOUND BY THE
PARTHENON PRESS, AT NASHVILLE,
TENNESSEE, UNITED STATES OF AMERICA

Foreword

THE HUMAN MIND AND SPIRIT, IN THE DAYS IN which we live, are subjected to great strain and pressure. The vicissitudes common to our humanity are always grievous and sometimes almost overwhelming. Then we have to reckon with the increased tempo of life in our day: its rush and excitement. The pace of life has become too much for its peace. The human spirit is being overborne. How portentous its problems are! How heavy is the burden of life! People are coming to feel that nothing can save them but a great incoming tide of spiritual energy that can lift them above the level of their fears and doubts. They cannot carry on at the present dismal level of hope. And in addition to all of this there is the burden of the world's present suffering and tragic disorder which perplex, bewilder, and depress the minds of all.

Under these conditions, it is no wonder that there has been a rapid increase in all sorts of mental and nervous disorders. How to help these sufferers has become one of the major interests of all those who are concerned with the sanity, the well-being, the happiness of men and women in our modern world.

5

A new department of medical science has come into being and wise psychologists and psychiatrists are alleviating the mental suffering of many and directing them into wholesome methods of thinking and living. There are, however, definite limits to a purely secular psychiatry, and even dangers in certain kinds of psychoanalysis whose merciless methods sometimes reduce the patient to a quivering mass of self-consciousness. The psychologist himself often recognizes the immense therapeutic value of religion and sends his patients where they may find it if he himself does not possess it and thus is not able to transmit it to them himself.

Thus the Church has begun to recognize its responsibility in this sphere of human welfare. It sees that

The generation in which we live is more delicate than its predecessors and looks for a Church which will help it back into spiritual health and give individual attention to the individual soul, recognizing the infinite variety of experience both healthy and diseased of which the individual soul is capable. From the beginning there has been this application of Christianity to spiritual failures. The Sacraments have been the source of spiritual life. There have been the priesthood and the confessional. But now for many generations the pulpit, the preaching of the word, and the practice of philanthropy have largely obscured the one thing needful—the care of the spiritually sick. The temptation of the clergy is to concern themselves too much with the preaching of faith and the practice of good works, to study too little the necessities of those whose souls are crying out for help.[1]

To this the Church is now giving increasing attention. Plenty of men, it has now come to understand, who serve parishes effectively by good preaching and skillful administration have neither the desire, the will, nor the ability to help men individually. Thus today candidates for the ministry are being trained in the principles of spiritual psychology and in personal relationships. They are serving terms in hospitals as internes. They are preparing themselves to exercise the high calling of the cure of souls. This, they are coming to understand, is the highest of all callings, and needs to be exercised with all the gifts that nature can bestow and with all the knowledge of moral and spiritual problems that training can give.

It would be a mistake, however, to imagine that

[1] Kirsopp Lake, *The Stewardship of Faith*, pp. 143, 144. Used by permission of the publishers, G. P. Putnam's Sons.

the opportunity for helping men in their mental and spiritual difficulties is confined to doctors and ministers. It lies within the reach of all strong and healthy people who themselves have discovered the secret of victorious living and are thus able to bring the influence of their own fortified personalities to bear upon the minds and spirits of those who are looking for direction and help. The possibility of thus mediating between the human soul and God is open to all who can win the confidence of others because of the authority of their own purity and because of their insight and their understanding of human need.

When we open the pages of the Gospels, we are made aware at once that Jesus moved into this broad area of human need with authority, with the word of hope and command. He confronted every type of physical, mental, and spiritual disorder. One can find the counterpart of all forms of suffering in our modern world in the Gospel stories, and we are able to discern the method of Jesus in dealing with them. Indeed, a careful study of this aspect of Jesus' ministry reveals that in this, as in every other sphere of life, he is the Master. Modern psychology has simply reproduced in its own fashion what we discern to have been the method of Jesus. It has perhaps unconsciously appropriated his own divine approach to the human problem.

The purpose of this writing is to disclose, by a careful study of the different varieties of human need as set forth in the Gospel stories, what the method of Jesus was, as a guide to our own dealing with men and women in mental and spiritual need. Thus this book may be useful to all who desire to be among those who can, to some degree, alleviate the suffering of their fellow men.

RAYMOND CALKINS

Cambridge, Massachusetts

CONTENTS

CHAPTER ONE

THE STRATEGY OF JESUS 13

CHAPTER TWO

NICODEMUS 36

CHAPTER THREE

THE WOMAN OF SAMARIA 54

CHAPTER FOUR

THE PARALYTIC 73

CHAPTER FIVE

"WHO TOUCHED ME?" 92

CHAPTER SIX

THE POOL OF BETHESDA 108

CHAPTER SEVEN

THE SYROPHOENICIAN WOMAN 129

CHAPTER EIGHT

THE RICH YOUNG MAN 145

CHAPTER NINE

THE BLIND MAN 164

CHAPTER TEN

ZACCHAEUS 183

CHAPTER ELEVEN

SIMON THE PHARISEE 200

THE STRATEGY OF JESUS

WHAT WAS THE SECRET OF THE MASTERY OF Jesus over the human soul? How are we able to explain, so far as such explanation is possible, his hold on the imagination and the affection of men, his control over their wills? An attempt to answer this question must render account first of the character, the person of Jesus himself, and then of his methods, his technique in dealing with men.

When we look at the Person of Jesus as it is exhibited for us on the pages of the Gospels, we are impressed at once with the graciousness, the kindliness, the innate refinement, courtesy, and delicacy of his spirit. Indeed, from this point of view, Jesus in perfect reverence has been called "the first of gentle-men."

The Gospel word for all of this is "grace." In its highest sense the word is used in the later New Testament for the absolute, unmerited, and over-flowing love of God. But in the Gospels, and applied especially to the Person of Jesus, the word denotes a certain attractiveness and charm, a beauty which covered him as with a garment of loveliness. He was "full of grace and truth" says the Fourth Gospel. "They wondered at the gracious words that proceeded out of his mouth." His approach to men always had within it and behind it this aesthetic quality of graciousness. And this impression of his grace "lingered like an aroma upon the minds of the Evangelists when they came to describe him as he was."

Anyone seeking to influence his fellow men needs to acquire this quality of "grace." Yet it is often overlooked, and for want of it many persons fail to win the confidence and response of those whom they seek to help. "Grace is not so much a duty done as a way of doing duty. It describes not so much a series of acts as the general radiation of a life. It is a beautiful way of doing things which proceeds from a beautiful soul." [1] Grace is not so much a virtue as an acquired instinct. "External manners may be cultivated to become what is called gracefulness, but graciousness is the unrestrained expression of the kindly self-forgetting and tranquil mind." [2]

[1] F. G. Peabody, *Jesus Christ and the Christian Character*, p. 193.
[2] *Ibid.*, p. 195.

14

Hence the importance that the grace that was in him should be the spiritual possession of all who seek to be the helpers of their fellow men. Much goodness, though it compels respect, repels affection. It is often careless of others' susceptibilities, undiscerning and lacking in insight and tenderness. On the other hand, there are people about whom there is an abiding sense of charm. Their characteristic quality is courtesy, insight, considerateness. "When one thinks of them, one recalls not so much their greatness as their grace." Such a quality cannot be learned, it must be acquired by a deep, inward spiritual process. The benediction of the grace of our Lord Jesus Christ must descend upon the soul. It takes, it has been said, three generations to make a gentleman. The third of these is surely the rebirth into the graciousness and beauty of character of Christ.

A second quality in the character of Jesus which gave him influence over men was the moral and spiritual power that was in him. In him was a deep fount of spiritual energy which, transmitted to other lives, gave them fresh vitality and reinvigorated them body and soul. When Jesus entered the arena of human living, this power at once manifested itself. The sick were healed; evil spirits were cast out of

15

men; the hopeless were given new courage; those bound by sinful habits were made free. In his poem "Christ in Hades," Stephen Phillips has described the effect of the entrance of Christ into the arena of the dead:

> Glimmering all the dead
> Looked upon Jesus; as they stood, some thought
> Spread from the furthest edges like a breeze,
> Till like a leafy forest, the huge host
> Whispered together, bending all one way
> Toward Him; and then ensued a silence deep.
> But suddenly the form of Jesus stirred;
> And all the dead stirred with Him suddenly.[3]

"As many as received him, to them gave he power," writes the author of the Fourth Gospel. It was the possession of this power that made men marvel at him; it was the transmission of this power that occupied him; it was the reception of this power that made men worship him.

The miracles of healing as they are recorded in the Gospels are no longer regarded as miracles, in the sense that the law which caused them is now well understood. Modern medical science has given

[3] From *Poems* by Stephen Phillips. Used by permission of the publishers, Dodd, Mead and Co.

this a name, psychotherapy. The power of the mind over the body is recognized today, and many a practitioner is healing diseases without the aid of drugs. Such was the power, the very life of God, in Jesus that, brought to bear upon the bodies as well as the souls of men, it gave health and life to those who were diseased. Nothing is clearer than that there came into this world with Jesus Christ a new, fresh, and incomparable moral power to re-create the lives of men.

No one is equipped to help others unless something of this inward power that was in Jesus is in him also. For it is only life that can touch life. There is no force in things to raise the sunken spirit, no balm in Gilead to cure the wounded will. Flame must be kindled by flame. It is the touch of man that heals. Psychologists and psychiatrists are agreed that we must get a new hope and sense of power into the lives of people if they are to get well and strong. They are also agreed that this new and quickened hope can be given only through the impact upon the life needing it by the life of one who possesses it.

There are people as we all know who in some strange way are able to make an instant and irresistible appeal to those with whom they come in contact.

17

Dr. William Osler possessed this power to a remarkable degree. His biographer thus describes the effect of his personality in a hospital ward:

All the unnecessary semblances of sickness and treatment were removed; it was turned from a sick room into a bright sunny room of repose. Then he started in with his patients. Very little medicine was given, to the astonishment of everyone. . . . . Under his stimulating and encouraging influence, the old cases nearly all disappeared, the new cases stayed but a short time. The revolution was wonderful. It was one of the most forceful lessons in treatment that had ever been demonstrated.[4]

And Osler himself was at pains to point out that the use of this power to arouse the soul to assert itself is not confined to physicians.

After all, faith is the great lever of life; without it man can do nothing. With it, even with a fragment, as a grain of mustard seed, all things are possible to him. We [doctors] never had, and cannot expect to have a monopoly in this panacea which is open to all, free as the sun, and which may make of everyone, in certain cases, "a good physician out of Nature's grace." If a

[4] Harvey W. Cushing, *Life of Sir William Osler*, I, 161, 162. Used by permission of the publishers, Oxford University Press.

poor lass, paralyzed, apparently hopeless, bedridden for years, comes to me, having worn out in mind, body, and estate a devoted family; if she in a few weeks or less by faith in me, and faith alone, takes up the bed and walks, the saints of old could not have done more. And we enjoy, I say, no monopoly of the faith business.[5]

If one asks whence comes this inward power, this secret of transforming and quickening influence, one can say only that it comes from the transmission into a human life of the very life of God. It is a divine afflatus and inbreathing of the spirit of God into a human life. It is the spiritual process whereby the life of God passes over into and becomes a reality in the life of another. And only to the degree that this has happened, and has thus equipped one with this secret power of influence can one hope to become a helper of one's fellow men.

A third element in the character of Jesus in his dealing with men was his sympathy. This too lies open on the pages of the Gospels. Everywhere we find instant, instinctive, outgoing sympathy. Bacon has said: "The nobler a soul is, the more compassion it hath." And Lessing has a word in his *Laokoon*: "Pity is the divinest emotion of the human heart." Few there are indeed who have not felt the stirrings

[5] *Ibid.*, I, 497.

19

of compassion. In Jesus we find this sentiment natural to the human heart exhibited in its highest and finest forms. Suffering in any form aroused his compassion. He never adopted, for example, the corollary so attractive to some spiritual enthusiasts that bodily suffering does not matter in comparison. It mattered enormously to him. The sight of bodily infirmity in any form moved him instantly. He never got used to it as we so often do. But, beyond this, life itself with its burdens of mind and soul as well as body seemed to him to be infinitely pathetic. A crowd always had a certain psychical effect upon his sensitive soul. "And seeing the multitudes, he was moved with compassion" by the realization of all the inevitable woe that was there presented to his mind and heart. The impersonal throng as well as the individual sufferer evoked his pity.

The sympathy of Jesus was continuous. It did not grow less and less as time went on, rather it seemed to increase. There was no diminution in its range and depth. It runs all through the story of his life from beginning to end. Once more, the sympathy of Jesus was constructive. It educated the will. His pity was not of the kind that weakens its object. It did not fall like a soft enervating influence on men. Rather it braced them, put them on their

20

feet. The sympathy of Jesus strengthened men's souls; it made for strong fiber. It made men ready for resistance and action. It was positive. It lifted men out of the slough of despond and the pit of hopelessness, their hearts filled with fresh faith and courage. Jesus walked boldly into a sphere of living which drags down where it does not degrade and spoke the word of hope and command.

Such, in general, are the characteristics of the sympathy of Jesus. And such must be the sympathy of all true helpers of men. Yet much that goes by the name of sympathy lacks these essential qualities. It is not intense. Often it is a sigh, an exclamation, a lamentation, but does not pierce to the center of one's nature and impel one to strong and sacrificial action. It is not continuous. While it may not be true that familiarity with suffering breeds contempt, it is true that it tends to breed indifference. It is not true that "to look upon the woes of men is sufficient to stir our pity in the extreme." Our sympathies tend to lose their edge and to become shopworn. It requires moral insight always to see the evil in the familiar. Also our sympathy is often debilitating and actually leaves the sufferer less prepared for struggle and resistance than he was. Too often it is a kind of pseudo sentimentalism which is in fact more cruel than strict justice. It hurts more than it helps. The sum total of the world's unhappiness is increased by the false sympathy of those who pride themselves on their sensitiveness to pain. There is nothing constructive in such sympathy. It does not equip the sufferer to grapple with his difficulties and overcome them. It is soft and enervating. True sympathy, by making short shrift of cowardice and self-pity, always summons the will to action. Modern therapeutics has taken this lesson straight from the Gospels and prescribes hard and even distasteful tasks to people who are unnerved and weak-willed through self-indulgence or despair of self. No disease is more fatal than self-pity, a malady that is attendant on an age of ease and the cult of pleasure. True sympathy always makes the sufferer forget himself and face duty with a resoluteness which releases unsuspected possibilities of self-recovery.

A final element in the character of Jesus in his dealing with men was his deep and abounding love. Jesus loved men, all sorts and conditions of men. This was his supreme passion. The story of this passionate love of men is written all over the pages of the Gospels. It has been the wonder of the world. The love which Jesus has evoked out of the human

her they were endlessly fascinating, endlessly appealing. In the unspoiled humanness of children she took long delight. She made no distinction between the humble and the famous, the rich and the poor. . . . . With the same joyous grace she welcomed a street-cleaner and a Prime Minister; a fish-peddler and a Governor or President.[6]

A third element in the love of Jesus for men was its insight, its perception of the deeper things in men, an intuitive knowledge of what they felt and needed and craved. His love, like the spiritual counterpart of a stethoscope, enabled him to detect the heartbeat of everyone with whom he came in contact. He was not incapable of severity where this was needed, of indignation and rebuke; but he was infinitely patient toward the defects in men because of his perception of the excellent in even uninteresting and apparently unpromising lives. Jesus' insight pierced beneath the most callous exterior. He put himself beside the soul that struggled to break its bonds whatever they might be. His discerning love won their confidence, and, undiscouraged by external obstacles, came down upon them "like rain upon the mown grass, as showers that water the earth."

[6] September 3, 1940.

The quality of an understanding and perceptive love is indispensable for all helpers of mankind. One said of Sidney Lanier that he could identify himself so completely with another's interests and so put himself on the same footing "that I quite forgot the difference in age and experience between us and almost felt him to be a companion student. He had the essential . . . . courtesy that was ready to transform interests by the alchemy of his touch."

Such, then, are the qualities in the character of Jesus in his dealings with men: grace, power, sympathy, love. In proportion as others derive these qualities from Jesus are they prepared to be the helpers of their fellows.

It is said of Jesus in the Fourth Gospel that "he knew what was in man." [7] Moffatt translates the verse: "He knew all men, and required no evidence from anyone about human nature; well did he know what was in human nature." The Gospels make very clear this capacity of Jesus to read men. He lived in the midst of a surging tide of humanity. All sorts and conditions of men came into touch with him; but, however casual the contact, he always seemed to know his man, he always put his finger on the right

[7] John 2:25.

26

spot, whether he had to deal with a shrewd lawyer, an outcast woman, or a Roman governor.

This accurate knowledge of men meant much for the work of Jesus. It gave a splendid and sane realism to his work. Jesus was a great idealist. And sometimes this truth is set forth in such a way as to imply that he was a mere dreamer. It is not so. He was a dreamer. But in his dreams and demands he never left the human plane. He knew the human material which he had to handle. He dealt with men as he knew them to be. How skillfully he handled every individual that crossed his path: Nicodemus, the woman of Samaria, the rich young ruler, the thief on the cross. He knew each one and led each one along the path that the individual case made imperative. It might be a difficult path; it was never an impossible one.

How much we need to learn this divine skill and strategy of Jesus in dealing with men! We often fail, fall short of our possible effectiveness, because of our short-sightedness and lack of knowledge and wisdom in our dealing with others. We are ignorant of their motives; we are blind to their possibilities; we bungle and blunder in our dealings with them. And thus we alienate them; we cannot get on with them; we do not understand them; we fail to help

27

them. How much it would mean if in our dealings with men we could acquire a tithe of the wisdom, the insight, the goodness, and the love of Jesus!

There are some people who have mastered this secret of Jesus. And see how influential they are. Behold how much good they do. There are some people who seem to understand. We go to them, and when we come away we say, "He read me like a book. For the first time, there is someone who just seemed to understand me." And how people do long to be understood! They do not even understand themselves. They yearn for someone who can interpret all the hidden complex of feeling, the rebellions, the contradictions of their own natures, and make clear to them what they are not able to make clear to themselves. And when they find a person who seems to see right through them, with the eyes of wisdom and insight, goodness and love, they feel for him unbounded gratitude and give to him their entire confidence.

And here is a mission to which we may all aspire. Here is something which, if we cultivate the qualities of which I have spoken, all of us, to greater or less degree, may be equipped to do. We talk of knowledge. What a wonderful thing it is to have knowledge. Yet we often overlook the highest

28

knowledge of all. There is no higher knowledge than the knowledge of men. We know so much. But do we know this? Do we know what is in men?

If we look a little more closely we discover something of the technique, of the method of Jesus in his dealings with men. For one thing, we note his keen observation. He could read the meaning of little signs, could see what they revealed of character. He was an expert in finding clues to personality in casual words and acts that disclosed to him the point of approach and enabled him to detect men's innate thoughts. How quickly and unerringly Jesus put his finger on the one determining factor in moral problems on which all else turned! No diagnostician ever went to the root and cause of disease more swiftly and accurately. Hence his decisions were immediate and final. One could accept them or reject them. But no one questioned them. For he knew what was in man. This ability to penetrate to the heart of moral situations and to give immediate direction to the questioner is one that is acquired only by experience, only by all the training that love of men can give. But once it is learned it lends great influence and gives great authority.

Again, how leisurely he was. There is no impression of haste. A certain serenity lies on the page. He

29

was never hurried. He seemed always to have ample time to deal with every human problem. We must imitate this method of Jesus in our dealings with men. All real helpers of men give this impression that they have plenty of time. How reassuring it is to the patient when the physician appears relaxed, at his ease, ready to listen indefinitely, and leaving only when the patient himself is relaxed and comfortable. To help men it is necessary at the outset to give them this assurance. People are sensitive to another's attitude. To appear in haste, to look at the clock, is to shut off at once the current of communication. Even if one feels that his time is limited he must never show it. He must reproduce the leisureliness of Jesus.

Once more we note the impersonalness of the attitude of Jesus. He appears detached, willing to give if he is needed, yet never looking for anything which the other is not ready to share. He does not force confidence, or seek to pry into men's secrets. He takes only what men are willing to give. He listens to what they are ready to say. Here, too, is something which all who seek to help their fellow men will do well to remember. There must be no hint of curiosity or of desire to get at what another may not be ready to reveal. At this point also suffering

souls are very sensitive. If one detects any reluc-
tance in another to tell the full story of his need,
one will say, "Perhaps you would rather wait; do not
go further if you would rather not." Any kind of
pressure brought to bear to force a confession which
another is not ready to make will cause the instant
loss of influence or power to reach and help. The
one fear which one will have in dealing with others
is that one should seem to wish to get any nearer to
them than they want one to get.

Frequently one will be importuned by a friend or
a parent to come to the assistance of one in need.
Always the wise method is to say, "I will, provided
he wants me and asks for my help." And because
one has once received another's confidence, one
must not assume that one is entitled to receive it
again. Perhaps the ideal of this kind of ministry is
best described for us by A. C. Benson in his essay on
Bishop Wilkinson:

He prayed and he blessed me and sent me away happy
and hopeful. He did not encourage me to come again
or to write to him, and I felt that he had no sort of
desire to establish a personal influence over me, but
rather let me fight my own battles on simple and
straightforward lines.

The problem which any soul presented to Jesus became at once the matter of his sole concern. It rose instantly into an isolated conspicuousness before his mind. It was as if this were the one problem with which he had to deal. No one who ever came to Jesus was made to feel that his trouble was petty and of minor importance. And if one is to help men, one must not only act as if this were so; one must feel that it is so. Any human problem must be given the dignity that belongs to it; and when one is dealing with it, it must become for the moment the most important and critical thing in the world. If one gives the impression by a smile or a shrug that this of course is a small matter, a minor incident among the more imperial interests of life, one will lose one's hold at once. It is not a small matter. It was not with Jesus, and it will not be with any true helpers of men.

No reader of the Gospels can fail to detect the note of severity in his dealings with men when the moral emergency seemed to demand it. Jesus was not only a gracious but a masterful personality of passionate energy who bent circumstances to his ends and wielded an immense authority over the wills of men. His words often sound like a peremptory command. They are like a bugle call to the timid and hesitant

32

souls of men. They are uncompromising in their demands. The shirker or the coward received no consideration at his hands.

It is a mistake to imagine that love and severity are exclusive terms. We have a lot of bogus love in the world. It is shallow, soft, and sentimental. But the love of Jesus is something different. His love of men is so profound that his warnings are sharp with the pain of it. The demands which he makes upon men summon their dormant wills to action, gear up their motives, put iron in their blood. None in the Gospels to whom Jesus was severe ever resented it. They knew that love was behind it. They knew that what they were bade to do was what they ought to do and what they could do.

And always Jesus believed in men, in their capacities, in their ability to rise above circumstance and sin and become the sons of God. He knew that underneath their failures and their discouragement, beneath their faults and their sin, there were reserves of strength and goodness and power of will; and he appealed to them, roused these people to fresh self-assertion, made them believe that by a new effort of their will they could and would rise to higher and better things. And thus he made better men and women of them. He saw something in them which others did not see, which they themselves did not see. His faith in them gave them faith in themselves, and was the beginning of their moral reformation. They acted on his belief in them, threw off their infirmities, and became free and strong.

We must imitate this divine strategy of Jesus in our dealings with men. We must believe that "in every human being lies the spark of immortal beauty to be fanned into flame by one rightly directed breath." [8] We take too low views of people. We dwell on their faults and their limitations. Our influence with people is in proportion to our faith in them. A mother can have great faith in a backward child and by her faith in him can make him self-reliant and strong. A friend can have great expectations for another doubting and melancholy friend whose will is weak and flabby, and by knowing what is really in him can make that will as taut as a bowstring. A wife can have faith in her husband who is discouraged and irresolute and thus give him initiative and courage. If a teacher cherishes high views of what his pupil can do, he can thereby help him to do it.

If, like Jesus, we can see beneath unpromising

[8] William J. Locke, *The Red Planet*, p. 339.

exterior and know what really is in people, like him we can make them what they may be and can be and ought to be.

Such, then, in briefest outline, are the methods of Jesus in dealing with men. The following chapters may be called "case studies," every one of which illustrates a different aspect of human need and Jesus' method in meeting it.

CHAPTER TWO

NICODEMUS

JOHN 3:1-15

GRAVE INJUSTICE HAS BEEN DONE TO THE character of Nicodemus. The common and conventional idea about him is that he was a timid and pusillanimous person, afraid to come to Jesus openly. So he came by night, in the dark, when the streets would be empty and he would be unseen. Moreover, when he got there he was not open and straightforward. He did not say, "I know"; he said, "We know." He impersonally hid himself behind others. Again, we are told that his attitude toward Jesus was patronizing. This inexperienced Galilean could not possibly understand the populace of Jerusalem, or be familiar with the peculiarities of those fickle and impressionable Judeans. So he had come to give Jesus needed counsel. It was as if he had said: "You are doing good work and God is giving you his blessing. But it would be better not to carry this too far. You may start something which will get beyond your control. I know the political situation pretty well. I advise you to go a bit more slow-

ly." And when he went away he was still uncon-
vinced. He had talked with Jesus. Yet he went back
and took his old place among the doctors. He had
heard a wonderful sermon preached by Jesus himself, and went on in the old way. Such is the picture of Nicodemus as it is usually drawn, the one
with which we are all most familiar. Yet I am convinced that it is not a true picture at all. I want
to take it down from our minds and memories, and
hang up in its stead the real portrait of Nicodemus,
the ruler of the Jews. It will repay us to study it.

Let us go back a bit. Jesus had come down from
Galilee to Jerusalem to attend the Passover. He entered the Temple area and found the money-chang-
ers and the grafters there. And the wrath of Jesus
was kindled, and he made a scourge out of small
cords and with flaming face drove them all out of
the Temple. Then for some days he stayed on, and
performed his works of healing and taught the people. And he made a deep impression. Many, we
read, believed in him. He had become an outstanding figure in the metropolis of the Jewish nation.
Among those who were impressed because of what
he said and did was Nicodemus. And consider for
a moment who Nicodemus was. In the first place,
he was a man of the Pharisees, of that party which,

with all its narrowness, pedantry, and agnosticism, still preserved a salt of genuine godliness and reared highly cultivated men like Gamaliel and Saul of Tarsus—and with these the name of Nicodemus must be linked. In the next place, he was a ruler of the Jews and a member of the Sanhedrin. If we take a university professor, a judge of the Supreme Court, and a bishop of the Church and combine these in one person, we have some idea of the kind of man Nicodemus was. He was a man of eminence, a leader in the ecclesiastical and political and intellectual world. When he passed along the streets of Jerusalem everybody knew him and honored him. And this was the man who came to Jesus. It was as if the president of a great university should go to a Salvation Army captain and should call him "Sir" and talk with him about religion. Even those who disparage the character of Nicodemus admit that it was a noble thing for him to do. It is true that he came by night, they say. But it is to his honor that he came at all.

That is more than a good many people today who are in the position of Nicodemus are willing to do. These people's minds are definitely and hermetically sealed against those spiritual values for which Jesus stands. They have not only made up their

38

minds, but they have locked them, and there is where the matter stands. Never since they became scholars and scientists and people of intellectual distinction have they sought out Jesus and sat at his feet and learned of him. All of this is outside of their sphere of interest. They never think of it at all. By contrast, we note what Nicodemus did and already we begin to admire him. At least he had an open mind. He was humble and teachable. He was not the victim of social pride or intellectual conceit. Here was something that challenged his attention. He determined to discover for himself the meaning of it.

It was Nicodemus, then, who came to Jesus, not Jesus who went to Nicodemus. Jesus went out of his way to call Levi the publican. He spoke first to the woman at the well. He made a special point of seeing Zacchaeus and of inviting himself to his house. But he set no account on this man's position or standing or influence. He did not go out of his way to seek Nicodemus, and it is not evident from what is written that he showed any exceptional eagerness in receiving his distinguished visitor or that he paid him any unusual attention. Such was the detachment of Jesus. Another might have thought that it was an event of some importance for the new

Teacher that one of Nicodemus' standing should come to him. Nicodemus may be pardoned if he cherished some such idea himself. But if so, the very first words of Jesus must have dispelled the illusion. And the relative position and attitude of the two never changed once during the entire interview.

The cause of a true religion is never furthered by any deference paid to position or station in life. The Church never gains ground by any form of obsequiousness to those who condescend to give it their attention. The Christian faith never thrives by seeking to accommodate itself to the contemporary mind or by compromising its essential truths in order to win the assent of a secular culture. The individual was never yet helped who felt himself to be on a higher level than the one who would help him. Always the relative position and attitude of Jesus and Nicodemus must be maintained if the truth for which Jesus stands shall find its vindication and produce its lasting results.

"The same came to Jesus by night." And why by night? The answer has been so long "for fear of the Jews" that one might almost think the words were in the text. But the words are not in the text.

They are used of Joseph of Arimathaea,[1] but they are never once used of Nicodemus. It is then a wholly gratuitous assumption to say that Nicodemus came by night because he was afraid to come by day. Moreover, what had he to be afraid of? Scribes and Pharisees were coming to Jesus openly all the time to ask him questions. And Nicodemus would have had nothing to fear had he come to him by day. People were doing it right along. Again, as all of his record shows, Nicodemus was far from being a timid man. Twice again his name is mentioned in this Gospel, and in each instance he shows himself to be a man of courage.[2]

Why then did he come to Jesus by night? The only natural inference is that he could not wait for day to come. Jesus had strangely attracted him. Some word of Jesus had entered his heart, some deed had awakened his wonder. The more he pondered, the less he was able to penetrate the mystery presented by the Person of Jesus. It was after dark; but the impulse to go to him at once was irresistible, and acting on it, night though it was, he came to Jesus. This should be remembered to his honor and not to his reproach. For Nicodemus came to

[1] John 19:38.
[2] John 7:50; 19:39.

Jesus in a deeper night than that which lay upon the outward world. He was in mental darkness and confusion. He could not see his way through the problem which Jesus presented to his mind. But Nicodemus did not wait for the day to dawn on all of these difficulties, and for all the dark mystery which encompassed him to be cleared up. In the darkness of his mental night, in the obscurity of unanswered questions, still he came. And what is clearer than that, if he had waited for the day to dawn he never would have come at all. But he came by night. And the light of a new day began to dawn the moment that he came into contact with Jesus. It may have been night when he came, but it was sunrise when he went away.

Thus, in coming by night, Nicodemus sets us in reality a high example of mental and moral courage.[3] There are many people today who are in the dark about Jesus. They cannot see their way. There are questions which they cannot answer. There is much which they do not understand. They feel that they must have more light on these matters before they can put themselves in any form of personal relationship with Jesus. I know of people who talked like that twenty years ago, and they are talking like that

[3] For a full development of this idea see Chapter II, "The Meaning of Faith," in the author's *Religion and Life*, Harper & Bros., 1935.

today. They will talk like that to the end of their lives unless they can make up their minds to act as courageously as Nicodemus did, and come to Jesus in their mental darkness and uncertainty. It is only in the light of his presence that they will see what today they cannot understand. If they wait to have all their questions answered before by an act of faith, believing that Jesus may be all that he claims to be, all that millions have found him to be, they put themselves into personal relationship with him, they will never come at all, and their questions never will be answered. But if, like Nicodemus, they will come by night, for them, as for him, day will begin to dawn.

Nicodemus, then, came to Jesus, and the interview began. The account of it is fragmentary. We do not know just how the conversation began or where it ended. A somewhat arbitrary line has been drawn at the fifteenth verse of this chapter. Enough has been included to make this scene forever solemn and unique.

"Rabbi, we know that thou art a teacher come from God." What a statement to come from the lips of one like Nicodemus! He called Jesus "Rabbi," a term of the highest respect. He said that not only he but many others in his position,

43

his friends and associates, had reached the same conclusion. We are reminded that in Jesus' day many
were his adherents, believers at heart, who did not
follow him as did the disciples. And the same is true
in our day. You cannot number the friends of Jesus
by a statistical statement of church membership.
Outside of those who have openly enrolled themselves
in the churches as his followers are many others who
know that Jesus is a Teacher come from God and
are following his example and seeking to walk in his
way of life. I pause, too, at the word "know." Now
Nicodemus was a lawyer. And a lawyer is always
careful how he uses the word "know." He will say,
"We have reason to believe"; or, "There are good
grounds for surmising"; or, "It is permissible to imagine." But he will never use the word "know" unless there is abundant and convincing proof. But
Nicodemus, with his legally trained mind, told Jesus
that he and many others like him were convinced
by overwhelming evidence that Jesus was a Teacher
come from God.

And if Nicodemus could say that in his day, who
is there among us who ought not to be able to say it
in ours? When Nicodemus made this statement
about Jesus and said "We know," the ministry of
Jesus had but just begun. Jesus had not yet shown

44

the reach of his power. Calvary and the Cross, the great manifestations of His Spirit—all these were in the future. But behind us lie twenty centuries of cumulative evidence of Jesus' mastership over the life, the conscience, the affection, the will of mankind. Can we not say at least this about Jesus: "We know that thou art a Teacher," not as other teachers, but a Teacher "come from God"? We know. We know by what we have read of him. We know by what we have seen of him. We know by what we have felt and experienced of him in our own hearts and lives, "for no man can do these miracles that thou doest, except God be with him." And whoever says that is not far from the Kingdom of God.

Not far from it, but still not within it. For to be in the Kingdom of God it does not suffice to believe something about Jesus, to stand off and admire him from a distance. To enter the Kingdom, one must surrender his life to Jesus; that the Life of God that was in him should pass over into and re-create the life of the believer into the Life of God. And this Jesus proceeded to say to Nicodemus.

It is not apparent that Jesus was surprised at Nicodemus' extraordinary confession. It is certain that he expressed no sense of gratification. Rather it was Nicodemus who must have been surprised. Whatever he might have expected that Jesus would say in reply, he could not have imagined that Jesus would say what he did: "Except a man be born again, he cannot see the kingdom of God." What a word to speak to a man like Nicodemus! He had everything that birth and breeding could give a man, and he was told that he must begin all over again. Had this been said to a poor outcast, to an ignorant or degraded sinner, the word would be comprehensible. But spoken to this cultured and righteous and intellectual aristocrat, this doctrine of a new birth must have come with stunning effect.

No wonder Nicodemus did not understand it. There are plenty of people today who do not understand it, and who will have nothing to do with it. It is still a stumblingblock to many who like Nicodemus have been bred in fine family tradition and in the intellectual discipline of the schools. To some it is a pure theological fiction; to others an opaque theological wonder; to still others an outworn theological tradition. And all of them regard it as the exclusive spiritual property of the uneducated religiously minded.

In comparison with these moderns, Nicodemus bore himself with singular courtesy and self-restraint. There is no hint of wounded vanity or of personal resentment in his reply. Neither was his answer evasive nor stupid nor flippant. On the contrary, he put his finger on the great, the apparently insurmountable difficulty. How can a man be born again when he is old? He cannot begin the process all over again from the day of his conception in his mother's womb and have the mysterious development repeat itself whereby characteristics are acquired, personality is formed, and that peculiar self which is a man has been attained. When a man becomes mature his destiny is told and he cannot alter it. That is what secular science is saying in our day. Medical science points to the difficulty of repairing old tissues; psychological science says that the groundwork of a man's character cannot be changed after he is thirty years old. He may execute little repairs, but by the time he is thirty he has built his house and he must be content to live in it. Similarly, the educationalists tell us that habits must be formed when children are young, for when they become old they cannot be changed. And sociologists speak of streams and tendencies which make for certain characteristics and have marks which are indelible and irremovable. Thus when Nicodemus said, "How can a man be born when he is old?" he was making a very profound and seemingly unan-

47

swerable reply to the saying of Jesus, "Except a man be born again."

We are now evidently in the center of a profound and critical inquiry, in which the whole place and meaning of religion in a man's life is involved. In the case of Nicodemus, Jesus was dealing with a type of person who was endowed with all that nature could bestow, who possessed all that external environment and natural inheritance could bequeath to a man. And in dealing with him, Jesus went to the root of the matter. In what he said to Nicodemus, he disclosed the fundamental principle of real religion, and the sphere and method of its operation. Nicodemus had much, yet what he had by inheritance and environment did not and could not of itself open to him the Kingdom of Heaven.

"That which is born of the flesh is flesh." Let nature have its swing, that is, and it will take him far in many ways, but it will not carry him into that spiritual realm in which are to be found the holiest attributes of character, the sense of profound fellowship with God, the sacrificial love for men and the peace and happiness that can surmount all obstacles, meet all vicissitudes in life. When one has been born into this world, whatever his inheritance and environment may be, he is not born into that.

48

NICODEMUS

To be born into a good family is not enough to put one into that kind of a Kingdom. If only a man could transmit the good that is in him and let the evil die there might be some hope that people could be bred into the Kingdom of Heaven. But alas! The taint in the blood is sent down with the virtue that is in it. Family connection, as we all know, is no guarantee of noble living. Without doubt the greatest peril to the state today is from the degenerate sons of noble families. To be born into a good environment does not mean that one is born into high and holy living. The outward circumstances of a man's life, however favorable, never yet spelt salvation of his soul. From the Garden of Eden down, the fall of man has taken place in many an earthly paradise. Education and culture of themselves do not put man into a spiritual Kingdom. Macaulay is authority for the statement that nine tenths of the evils that afflict the human race come from a union of high intelligence and low desire. Always and everywhere the trained mind becomes a danger and a menace unless it is guided and inspired and held to noble ends by motives which mental training can never generate. And always, even when inheritance and environment have done their best for a man, there is the danger that pride and self-

complacency and self-righteousness, deadliest foes of
a man's higher nature, will stand between him and
the Kingdom of Heaven. In a word, the secular can
never produce the spiritual. The divine can never
be evolved out of the human. "That which is born
of the flesh is flesh." It is a fundamental proposition
which was given a dramatic illustration in the person of the flesh-born Nicodemus.

"Do not wonder at my telling you that you must
be born again from above. For if what is born of
the flesh is flesh, it is also true that what is born of
the Spirit is spirit." No matter who or what you are,
operating independently of age and condition, there
is always the infinite and imminent possibility that
this reconciling power, this strong and irresistible
stream of life, the very Spirit of God, may sweep
through your nature like a cleansing stream, break
through every obstacle of habit, prejudice, or acquired characteristic of nature, bring to life every
dormant purpose and impulse, and re-create the inner man into the very image of God. "The Spirit
blows where it wills." By a thousand different ave-
nues it finds its way into a man's life. Something
makes him serious and thoughtful; the shadow of
a divine discontent falls gently on the landscape of
his thoughts and moods; visions of a nobler life pass

before him beckoning and calling. But these are intermittent. These come and go like flitting twilight shadows. These are not the standing possession that we seek. Where shall we seek for it? Where, indeed, but in the touch upon our natures of some nature that is purer, better than our own. The highest regenerating influence on earth comes from holy human lives. The great poets have all felt this. The central idea in the greatest poems of the language is the redemption of the human soul through the power of another human life—as in Browning's *The Ring and the Book,* where the gay young priest, with none too keen a conscience, with all his thoughts of life and conduct perverted by the low standards of his day, is redeemed by contact with Pompilia, the whitest, purest, womanliest soul in fiction, whose regenerating influence is one of the most beautiful incidents in literature.

And it is but one step from the recognition of the redemptive power of a human personality, to the recognition of the universal power over other lives of that one universal and sinless life which, from the day when his Presence and Person first began to fix men's eyes upon him, to touch their hearts, resuscitate their consciences, to awe and subdue their wills, down to the very day in which we live, has not ceased to do for the moral life of men what no other life that ever lived on earth has been able to do.

This was the truth which began to dawn upon the soul of Nicodemus, the beginning of the sunrise of his life. It subdued him, awed him, opened up new vistas of living of which he had never dreamed. "How is all of this possible?" And then Jesus pointed out the way to this total regeneration of the soul by pointing to himself. "As a teacher of Israel, this should not be difficult for you to understand, for all the Scriptures in which you are versed have contained within them the hope, the prophecy of the coming of One in whom the very Life of God should be revealed for the redemption of man. If you have found difficulty in understanding this life as it has manifested itself in purely human spheres of action, no wonder that you should be slow in apprehending its meaning in the innermost life of the soul. Yet that is the truth, the final truth which I have come into the world to hold before the souls of men. Precisely as Moses lifted high in the desert the serpent, seeing which men should not die, even so when I am lifted high above all else, everyone who trusts in me shall have eternal life."

So Jesus dealt with Nicodemus. The sequel of

the story is left untold. For myself, I have no difficulty in reconstructing it. Everything that I read of Nicodemus in this chapter reveals a reverent, humble, open-minded and courageous spirit, sensitive to truth and capable of obeying it. He had come by night unable to understand who and what Jesus was. He went away in the daylight of the truth that in Him was the revelation of that Life to which he himself, with all of his distinction and culture, of himself could never hope to attain. Only a little later we find Nicodemus standing up before the sneering, cruel Sanhedrin, pleading that fairness and justice be shown this Galilean whom they, with their lost, respectable souls, were hounding to death. Later still, at the very last, we find him bringing spices and fine linen to wrap in them the body of his Lord and to anoint it for the burial. Nicodemus had entered the Kingdom of Heaven.

CHAPTER THREE

THE WOMAN OF SAMARIA

JOHN 4:1-22

THE STORY OF JESUS' INTERVIEW WITH THE woman of Samaria may be called a Gospel within the Gospel. Almost every aspect of the faith of Jesus may be found within it. The story itself is so simple and transparent that one is likely to forget that there is anything remarkable about it. It is only as one studies its separate features and lets one's mind rest on the different aspects of this simple scene that one discovers its depths, and draws from it, as the story itself says, the living water.

Samaria lay right across Palestine from the sea to the river Jordan. Jews, too scrupulous to pass through Samaritan territory, were thus obliged to cross the Jordan twice, and to make a considerable detour. Jesus, however, took the stright northern route, passing into Samaria, until he came to Sychar and the well of Jacob, where it was natural for the tired traveler to rest at noonday.

We first read about Jacob's well in the book of Genesis, and it exists to this day. It is one of the undisputed localities associated with the life of our Lord. The modern traveler may sit on the rim of the well as Jesus did, and a priest of the chapel built about it will let down a bucket into the water which has not ceased to flow for these thousands of years. And the well is indeed very deep.

"Then cometh a woman of Samaria to draw water: Jesus saith unto her." How simple and natural it sounds. If we think of it at all, we think only of the delicacy of Jesus' words to her. But doubtless what most impressed the disciples on their return from the neighboring village of Sychar, where they had gone in search of food, was that Jesus should have spoken to her at all. For one thing, this was not according to oriental forms of etiquette. For another thing, she was a Samaritan. And a good Jew would never speak to a Samaritan, man or woman. When therefore Jesus at noonday entered into conversation with this woman, he violated all the social standards and conventions of his day. And he did it very simply, very naturally, as if he were not at all aware that his conduct was in any way sensational or out of the ordinary. So oblivious was Jesus to the artificial distinctions of race or society. He plumbed beneath all of these and dealt with men on the deeper level of their common humanity.

Here we find in miniature Jesus' solution of one of men's most vexing problems: how human beings are to live together. People who have skins of one color do not want to live with people whose skins have a different color. Or people whose skins have the same color do not want to live with each other because they do not speak the same language or occupy different strips of territory. Or people talking the same language and living in the same land cannot get on with each other because they differ in birth or wealth or culture. Thus we face the race problem, the national problem, the social problem. But with Jesus it was no problem at all. These divisions that separate man from man for him did not exist. All men for him stood on the same level because one was their Father, even God, and thus they were brothers. When Jesus spoke quite naturally at noonday with this Samaritan woman, he condemned the artificial and cruel organization of human society and pointed to the day when a true spiritual democracy would take its place.

Anyone can test his own competency to be a true helper of his fellow men by asking himself to what degree racial and social prejudice still controls his thought and feeling, to say nothing of his actions, in relation to those with whom he comes in daily contact. Only when one is both uninfluenced by these and also quite simply unconscious of them, can one deal with men on the deep levels of their common needs and equal capacities as the children of God.

We note, as we read the conversation, that profound truth was uttered by Jesus to this poor and unknown woman. Here are some of the greatest words which ever fell from his lips: "Whosoever drinketh of the water that I shall give him shall never thirst; but the water that I shall give him shall be in him a well of water springing up into everlasting life." "The hour cometh, and now is, when the true worshippers shall worship the Father in spirit and in truth." "God is a Spirit: and they that worship him must worship him in spirit and in truth." Surely, one says, the audience was not worthy of the discourse. Such an utterance deserved the largest and the most appreciative company of listeners. To speak such immortal words into the ears of one dull and unintelligent woman was poor economy of resource. Did not Jesus himself teach that while one must not judge harshly on the one hand, he should be discriminating on the other, distinguish between the characters of those with whom one has to do, and not cast pearls before swine? Yet is he not doing just that in talking thus to this one uncomprehending mind?

As a matter of fact, we wholly misinterpret this well-known saying of the Sermon on the Mount if we find an illustration of it here. There Jesus was simply qualifying the injunction to merciful judgment, by pointing out that there are cases of moral turpitude where condemnation and not extenuation is demanded; where the pearls of mercy would be scorned and treated with contempt by those to whom they were cast. But Jesus never thought that any needy soul, however worthless in man's eyes, was unworthy of the divinest things he had to give. Here we touch another of the methods of Jesus in dealing with men. There was never economy of resource. There was never a withholding of the uttermost he had to give. He lavished all that he was and had to feed the hunger of one solitary soul. The method of Jesus for redeeming this world was not to wait for great occasions or for some dramatic moment. Rather it was to utilize any opportunity that came to him in the most ordinary, commonplace, and out-of-the-way events of everyday life, and then to give all that was most precious to the one soul who needed it. He was tired. He rested. A woman came. He said, "Give me to drink." A conversation ensued. A soul was redeemed. That was the method of Jesus. What was clearer than that this poor soul in her life of dull monotony, of helpless commonplace, of sordid sinfulness needed a well of water within her that should spring up into everlasting life. And Jesus gave her that. And for that, his best was none too good.

By contrast, we think of how we are wont to save our best for the best—the best moment, the best occasion, the best people. We hesitate to squander, as it seems, our highest inspirations on the small occasion, on the few, on the less appreciative or the less deserving. When shall we learn that the measure of what we give is never the worth but the need of those to whom we give it? The real helpers of men never pause to calculate the relative worth of those to whom they minister and give accordingly. The real surgeon will utilize the utmost of his skill upon one from whom he never expects any remuneration. The real teacher will employ all of his experience and patience and knowledge in helping some unrewarding pupil out of his bewilderment and discouragement. The true social worker will give days of his time in helping to his feet one who may never make any success in life at all. The secret of influence is to be lavish of one's self. And the time to be lavish of one's self is not in hours chosen by us, but in hours chosen for us. The redemption of the world waits upon the bestowing of the best effort of which we are capable, upon those with whom we are thrown into contact in the casual happenings of everyday life. Often as we pause in some incidental way on our daily path, or stop for a moment's rest in the business of life, we come face to face with someone who uncovers in a casual word his spiritual need or loneliness or emptiness. That is the moment, that is the place for us to do our most and to give our best.

How delicately and deftly Jesus led the conversation on from what was immediate and material to the spiritual truth which he saw was that woman's deepest need. He began by asking a favor of her, a drink of water. It was a familiar method of Jesus in dealing with people whom he was about to help, to ask them to help him. We shall find other illustrations of it. It is a sure way of gaining attention and of winning response. The appeal to another on the basis of his need does not always succeed. One may not be conscious of his need, and he will not pretend to feel what he does not feel. Or there may be an inward withdrawal as from one who proposes to give a benefit to one who is not sure that he wants it. The passive acceptance of something given does not rouse the will, stir enthusiasm or command interest, whereas the request for help does just that. It is a principle which can be carried into many relationships in life. The child who is uninterested and inattentive so long as his father is trying to amuse him, becomes alert and responsive at once when the suggestion is made that he can help his father. The pupils who are restless and listless while their teacher is asking them to absorb what he has to give, become awake and alert at once if they are asked to co-operate with the teacher in seeking the solution of some problem. Always this is the appeal that carries. And Jesus makes frequent use of it in his dealings with men. When he asked this woman to give him a drink of water, he won her interest as he could have won it in no other way.

I pause here to remark that in a profound way this woman, poor and ignorant as she was, had it in her power to give a gift to Jesus, as truly as he had it in his power to give the gift of life to her. She did indeed give him to drink, for he thirsted for the souls of men, and every life redeemed from sin was as water to his soul. The response of any life

61

to what he had to offer was the deepest of all joys to Jesus. When the day was over the woman's life was different from anything it had been. But the heart of Jesus was made glad also, even as there is joy in heaven over one sinner that repenteth. A fact often overlooked by those who are helped by others is that they have really done more for their helpers than these have done for them. No one who has ever succeeded in touching the hidden springs in another's life, thus awakening it to new possibilities of being and living, will fail to recognize this truth. What one receives in being able to help men is always more than one gives.

In another way also this woman had ministered to Jesus. For she brought forth from his heart the living water of which this chapter so eloquently speaks. From this point of view, there is hardly a person in all the Gospels who performed such a service as this one passive and apparently dull and unresponsive auditor. The very fact of her seeming impenetrability made its deep appeal and called forth the uttermost that Jesus could give. Some of the greatest words that Jesus ever spoke were evoked from his heart by the stark emptiness of her life. If it is true that the strong make the weak, it is no less true that the weak reveal the strength of the strong. One who cannot himself do great things may be the cause of other people doing them. No helper of men but is himself at his best when he confronts humanity at its worst.

But let us come back to this immortal conversation and see how it developed. In reply to Jesus' request for a drink of water, the woman expressed surprise that he, being a Jew, for she recognized him as such at once, should be willing to talk to her as familiarly as he did and to ask a favor of her. "For the Jews have no dealings with the Samaritans." At this point Jesus gives the conversation its turn to interests deeper and more spiritual. It is done very simply and naturally. "If you but knew what God has to give, and how able he who speaks to you is able to give it, you would have asked him and he would have given you living water." This word of Jesus is the turning point in the whole story. He made swift use of the analogy of physical thirst to point to the soul's thirst for God. He reached at once for the heart of the woman. He utilized the simple human situation to show her the way to God. With unerring intuition he penetrated beneath immediate circumstance to the deep and central need of her life. All true helpers of men have the same insight, the same skill to transform

a simple, natural occasion into a moment of deep
spiritual meaning. Years ago Dr. Theodore Cuyler
of Brooklyn was talking to a friend who came into
his home during a heavy thunder shower. The
man was no churchgoer, took scant interest in the
religious aspects of life. He had a son whom he
loved dearly. "I am afraid," he said, "that my boy
is out in all this storm. He is not strong. It will
do him no good." Quick as a flash Dr. Cuyler replied: "It seems a bit strange to me that you should
be concerned for his health, yet should apparently
have no anxiety that he should have that deeper
protection that only religion can give." And that
one word proved to be a decisive moment in the
man's life.

The woman of Samaria had no inkling of what
Jesus meant, and asked in all literalness how Jesus
could give her to drink when he had nothing to
draw with and the well was very deep. Unwittingly
the woman had uttered a profound truth. Jesus
had indeed nothing visible or material with which
to draw. He relied on none of the means common
to men in order to attract them to himself. The
only attraction of Jesus is the Person of Jesus. Yet
how irresistible this has proved. "I, if I be lifted
up . . . . , will draw all men unto me." He had

nothing to draw with except himself. Yet who in the long range of history has ever attracted and attached men to himself like Jesus?

The supremely attractive thing in any man is simple holiness. In our efforts to interest others and to influence them, we often forget this. We think of the drawing power of beauty, of fascination, of intellect too, or wit or what we call personality. Yet none of these can compare with the drawing power of a life of goodness, disinterestedness, and love. It is not enough to be only religious. "There are some whose religion has every quality but one— attractiveness. They are animated by the sincerest motives, they are ruled by the tenderest conscience, they are influenced by the purest desires, yet their religion is not . . . . a magnet in the heart." [1] They do not have in them the beauty of holiness. That was the supreme drawing power of Jesus. He had nothing else, but he had that. And to attract men as Jesus did, it is necessary that one have this in- dispensable possession. To share the spirit of Jesus enables one like nothing else to draw men unto one's self.

Jesus went on. Only now he spoke more directly and personally. "Drink of this water, and you will

[1] George Matheson, *Moments on the Mount*, pp. 273-274.

thirst again. But drink of the water that I shall give, and it will be a constant well of water spring-ing up so that a man will never thirst again." And the dull and unimaginative woman, tired of having to come to the well to draw water, thinking that here perhaps was some magician, asked for this miraculous water.

Then, suddenly and without warning, Jesus plumbed to the depth of her heart. "Go, call your husband." He had touched at once the center of her whole moral need, the sordidness of her ex-istence. In a moment she perceived that she was face to face with One who knew her. It is not necessary to assume that in thus telling her who and what she was, Jesus was exercising any extraordinary powers of prescience, or that "seven" meant more than a round number of her husbands. To Jesus' penetrating mind the character of the woman stood revealed. He uncovered it at once and gave her to understand where lay the secret of her innermost need. Here Jesus was the spiritual surgeon. If she were to recover spiritual health, the disease which corrupted her life must be cleanly and com-pletely removed. Only so could she put her feet in the pathway of self-recovery. Here there could be no evasion, no compromise.

There are many illustrations of this method of Jesus in his dealings with men. The irradication of moral evil is a necessary preliminary to future spiritual development. The spiritual life cannot in any real sense be lived unless virtue lies secure and solid at the base. The superstructure must lie on firm and sure foundations. Jesus always insisted on this. He was never so eager to have one become a disciple that he was willing to overlook moral weakness, whatever it might be. True helpers of men always imitate this method of Jesus. They uncompromisingly insist that wrong habits shall be recognized as such and shall be wholly and completely abandoned. They do not excuse or extenuate, or consent to any halfway measures. Reformation must be from the bottom, and it must be final. It is interesting to observe that the wrongdoer himself respects and responds to this attitude. In his heart he approves it, feels its sanity and justice, and actually prefers such treatment to a more lenient and easy-going judgment. He will respond to a stern summons to break with his past, rally his forces, and begin anew. Palliative measures do not meet his case, and in his heart he knows it.

Teachers and preachers of religion will do well to hold to this inexorable requirement of Jesus that a thoroughgoing morality lie at the basis of a subsequent and higher experience of the religious life. When Jesus said that the righteousness of his disciples must exceed that of scribe and Pharisee he plainly implied that this righteousness must include it. Ordinary everyday virtue and morality is the presupposition of higher Christian living. Nothing would perhaps do more to rehabilitate Christianity in the minds of many people today who are frankly critical of the Christian community than to have its members exhibit the righteousness of every last scribe and Pharisee in their midst. If men could see Christian people giving undeniable evidence that they possess the fundamental virtues, making these the starting point for a higher kind of living, more people would be attracted to the higher living for which Christianity stands. What often brings Christianity into disrepute in the modern mind is the spectacle of men and women talking about grace and faith and the rare experiences of the Spirit who yet have failed to incorporate in their moral make-up the virtues of honesty, generosity, courage, and loyalty essential to true and noble living. Some people, it has been said, present the appearance of having been starched before they have been thoroughly washed. Jesus always began at the beginning. If one would not rectify what was wrong at the center of his life, he was not qualified to go further. A thoroughgoing education in moral values, uncompromising in its demands, making for sincerity in every department of life, is a true imitation of the methods of Jesus in dealing with men.

Again the woman was slow to understand. Jesus must be a mind reader, a soothsayer; she called him a prophet. And she reminded him in her unimaginative way that as a prophet he was outside his jurisdiction, since for the Jews religion was restricted to Jerusalem. This called forth from Jesus one of his greatest words, in which he broke down and broke through all conventional religious ideas and announced the universal scope and meaning of all real religion: God is a Spirit who is truly worshiped not in one place rather than another but wherever and whenever he is worshiped in spirit and in truth.

Here a ray of light seems at last to have pierced the dark mind of his listener. For she answered: "Even we Samaritans believe that the Messiah will come, and when he does he will instruct us in all of this." And swiftly Jesus answered: "You do not need to wait. I that speak unto thee am he."

The disciples returned from Sychar. The interview was at an end. The spiritual sequel is left to the imagination. The woman, we read, leaving her pitcher, forgetting in the newness of this revelation that for which she had come, went back home and told her friends what had befallen her and said, "Is not this the Christ?" And they all went out and came to him.

Consider what that one day meant to this unknown Samaritan woman. What could have seemed more unlikely to her, trudging out to her well that day which looked like all the rest of her days, with no sign about it that anything unexpected was to happen, than that words were to be said to her that were to change the whole current of her life and cause herself to be remembered to the end of time? For the light which that day began to burn dimly, we must believe burned more and more brightly until her whole existence was illumined and transformed by it. Her path intersected just for a moment with the path of Jesus. But that moment was critical, it was decisive, and all her life was irrevocably altered by it. That day she received the gift of God. She could not have known all that it meant; but it meant enough to be for her a well of living water and it sprang up within her into ever-lasting life.

And what was it? Negatively it was just the knowledge of herself. Jesus made her aware of her need. But positively what was it? In all the after days of her life what was the well of living water within her? If the question be pressed, it will be seen that it must have been just the remembrance of Christ, the knowledge that in him God had sought her and claimed her in the midst of her evil life for some better and holier thing, had indeed loved her through her sin and had sent deliverance to her. That knowledge still is and always will be the living water to every soul of man.[2]

In some such way all true helpers of men bring salvation to others. Against the background of their own pure and fortified lives, these are made to feel their own helplessness, weakness, and need. And the goodness, patience, insight, and ceaseless love of those who seek to help them to better things evoke a strong and passionate response. All that is best is called to life. The remembrance of it remains a constant inspiration. "I shall spend all my life," so wrote a woman to one who had tried thus

[2] From a Sermon by Francis G. Peabody, published in pamphlet form under the title, *The Water of Life.*

to befriend her, "trying harder than you know to be all that you could hope for me to be." Disinterested love of others derived from Jesus who himself derived it from God is indeed living water to men's souls. It is not a little stream that soon runs dry. To the end of their lives it comes as fresh and reviving as at the first and it has the same power of supplying motive to men's lives as it had when Jesus talked that day to this unknown woman of Samaria.

CHAPTER FOUR

THE PARALYTIC

MATTHEW 9:2-8; MARK 2:1-12; LUKE 5:18-26

WE SHALL NEED TO USE ALL THREE ACCOUNTS
of this story in order to reconstruct it for ourselves.
The incident occurred in the early days of the
ministry of Jesus, while he was staying at Caper-
naum at the home of Peter. And it was noised
about that he was in the house. For already the
fame of Jesus had spread, and particularly his fame
as a healer. That was quite natural. But it was
not as a healer primarily that Jesus wished to be
known. Have you sometimes wondered why Jesus,
after he had healed some poor sick person, admon-
ished him to keep this to himself and to tell no man?
He was anxious lest people should look upon him
chiefly as a worker of miracles. Yet human nature
then as now craved deliverance from disease. And
already he had cast an evil spirit out of a man, and
healed Peter's wife's mother of a fever, and even
cleansed a leper. And we read that Jesus could no
more enter into a city, and that they came to him
from every quarter. So, when it was known that

he was in the house of Peter, a great crowd gathered at once.

Well, here was a poor paralytic, a young man. It was a pathetic sight then, and it is today. All power of locomotion gone, he lay helpless on his bed. And here were four friends, or it may be relatives, determined to bring him to Jesus. One of the most touching things in the Gospels is this solicitude of people for their families and their friends: Jairus for his daughter; the centurion for his servant; Mary and Martha for their brother. You can find the same thing in the world today, and it is always a beautiful thing to see.

Now observe what these four men did. Love always prompts to action. No obstacles could prevent them from getting their friend to where Jesus was. They heard that Jesus was staying at the house of Peter. They knew where he lived. So they carried the man there on his litter. But when they got near, they found not only a house full, but the street full of a jostling crowd of people, trying to get near Jesus to hear what he was saying and to watch what he was doing. Of course, they might have left the sick man on the outside and elbowed their way in and pleaded with Jesus to heal him. But no! They must place him right before Jesus,

74

before those eyes of love that never could rest on human misery without compassion. So they did a sensational thing. In some way they got him to the roof of the house, broke through it and let him down to the very feet of Jesus.

In order to understand how this was done we must remember what houses in the East are like. Peter's house was not likely to be any grand affair, probably of one story only, built around the four sides of a little courtyard, open to the sky. But if the owner of the house desired more room it was a very simple thing to cover in the courtyard by the process of putting planks across from one side to the other, not more than ten feet from the ground, covered with tarpaulin or straw matting, so that in the center of the house he had a large roomy space, not rainproof perhaps, but sunproof, where he could offer accommodation for a considerable number of people.

So we can imagine what happened when this boy was brought to the house. These men had a tremendous faith that if only they could get him to Jesus he would be healed. So they pressed their way through the crowd until they got to the stone stairway that always leads from the street to the flat roof of a house in the East. They managed to get their stretcher up on the roof. Then they removed the covering and the planks and with ropes they let down the bed on which the helpless man lay into the midst of the crowd, and right before where Jesus stood. These four men then for love's sake did that sensational thing. No wonder Jesus admired it. They had that tremendous faith. Duty would have bade them place the mat on the edge of the crowd and hope for the best. But faith prompted them to climb to the housetop and dig through the roof.

And there is always a roof that we must break through. For Jesus is still in a building, within four walls and under a roof. The essential Christian Idea is that in Jesus Christ is compacted the life and love of God that is able to save the bodies and souls of men. But around that Idea have been necessarily built walls and roof to contain it. That Idea has been embodied in outward and visible forms that are the work of men's hands. A religion necessarily gathers about itself a theology, a creed, a system, an organization, a liturgy. And all of these have their importance. But the danger always is that these shall be regarded as the real thing. And they are not. The real thing is God-made and God-given. And these things are man-made.

They are only the walls and the roof within which the real thing which is Christ himself is to be found. And if we are to find Christ himself we must break through all of that; break through the outward systems and doctrines and creeds—the human effort to encase the reality in outward form—we must break through all of that and come to Jesus himself. The reason and the only reason why multitudes of people never discover the power that is able to save them or their friend's body and soul is that they are kept from him by the roof that is over his head. But these men "uncovered the roof where he was: and when they had broken it up, they let down the bed wherein the sick of the palsy lay" to where Jesus was. And if the rest of the story is to be true today, we must do likewise. We must get our paralyzed friends, we must get our paralyzed selves to Christ himself.

And now we get on with our story. Try to imagine how this poor boy felt, coming down on his mat lowered by the ropes. He was let down in front of a crowd of people. If he looked one way he looked into the hard and pitiless eyes of the Pharisees, who were watching to see if Jesus would dare to heal him on the Sabbath day. But when he turned the other way he saw Jesus, who looked

77

up at those friends on the roof and then upon him with eyes that were searching but full of understanding and tenderness and sympathy and love.

Now Jesus had been speaking. There was such a crowd that we read that "there was no room to receive them, no, not so much as about the door." But when the boy arrived the sermon came to an abrupt end. Jesus turned aside from the crowd to attend to the one. He was always doing that. And therein lies the difference between Jesus' methods and ours. We attach great importance to crowds. We estimate the success of a church service by the number of people there are present. We count the congregation. The size of the "audience" is the test. But it was never the test with Jesus. He never cared for a crowd. Over and over again he turned aside from a crowd to help one person. So the paralytic had his entire attention. The crowd had to wait. Surely, thought the crowd, that was the wrong way about. The sick man ought to be the one to wait. What an audience! What an opportunity, one that ought not to be lost! But it is the glory of the New Testament the way God cares for the one. "He careth for you," says Peter. One sick soul claimed all his attention. And that church service was a success not because of the crowd that was in it, but because that one man was in it. A church may be crowded today. But if no paralyzed person has been made to walk, the fact that a crowd has been in it counts for nothing.

There the boy lay at the feet of Jesus. "When Jesus saw *their* faith. . . . ." It was not the faith of the patient, it was their faith, the faith of his friends. But it was faith just the same. Jesus can do nothing without faith. It is only in the atmosphere of faith that his healing can be wrought. This poor boy may not have had much faith. But his friends—they had tremendous faith. Read the Gospels through, and whenever you find Jesus healing anyone, there you will find the word faith. And when faith is absent there is no miracle. When the scribes and the Pharisees asked him for a "sign," he said that never should be given them. But *faith* even as small as a grain of mustard seed was sufficient. And this faith that was a prerequisite to healing—what was it? Just this tremendous conviction: that Jesus had the power to make a man whole. Probably that sufferer had lost hope. He had lost faith in himself. His self-confidence was all gone. He had ceased to believe in the possibility of his recovery. But the faith that he lacked was supplied by his friends. They positively refused to give him up. They believed that there was something there. They continued to believe when the man had ceased to believe in himself. And that is where we can all begin if we have some paralyzed friend. Was it not Galsworthy who said, "I think the greatest thing in the world is to believe in people"? For if we believe in our friends they will react to that belief and become what we believe they can be. If there is one reflection that holds a man firm and keeps him straight, it is the belief in him on the part of those who love him. It is a tremendous support to one whose self-confidence has been shaken to know that someone else all the time continues to believe in him. It helps him to believe in himself.

These four men, then, continued to believe in the possibility that their friend could recover, and vicariously they supplied the faith necessary for his healing. And if we have some paralyzed friend it is an immense inspiration to remember that we can do so also. Our love can create the conditions under which the divine energies may be released and may operate. Someone whom we love may have ceased to hope, ceased to pray for himself. But by our prayers of faith we can set God's great healing powers to work. Thus our task in dealing with others is

80

to supply the faith that they may not themselves possess. The one and only thing that we can truly say about prayer and faith is, that we do not know the breadth of the limits within which they can operate. Prayer does not tell God anything which he does not konw. Neither does it persuade him to come to the rescue. But it does supply the soul of the sufferer with what it needs in order that the power of God can do its perfect work. Just as asceptic conditions are necessary to the surgeon, without which he can do no mighty work, so again and again we help people by surrounding them with all the energies of God. Medical science and modern psychology alike recognize the therapeutic value of the prayer of faith.

After Jesus had looked up at those men, and had understood what they had done, and had seen their faith, their passionate hope and longing and expectation, then he turned to the poor boy lying there and spoke to him. Two of the evangelists report that he addressed the boy as "My son"; Luke has it "Man," or "Friend." Neither gives the real sense. The Greek word is "child." It is a term of endearment. Perhaps the words "My child" will come as close to it as any other. But, to the boy's surprise and probably to the surprise of his friends, Jesus

81

said nothing at all to him about his legs, nothing about his paralysis only. He got down deeper than that. "My child, your sins are forgiven." Jesus saw that the root of the trouble lay in the soul of the sufferer. We touch here an obscure, but what is coming more and more to be recognized as a pathological fact: that a sense of sin in one form or another sometimes does underlie disease, and that to cure the disease all that is necessary is to remove the malady of the spirit. We shall come across this again in these chapters. All kinds of physical illness, medical science is discovering, have no physical cause whatsoever. There is a guilt-complex somewhere in which fear is alive, and this produces the paralysis of some bodily function. The root trouble lies in some disharmony between soul and body. We call this a complex or a neurosis, the failure on the part of the patient to adapt himself to the difficult business of living. And every day in our modern world people are being healed by going away down into their spiritual being. A man or a woman labors under the sense that he has neglected his filial duty; or he has gotten into a panic about certain kinds of sin, fearing that that secret sin will have some terrifying consequence. So he develops a guilt complex and this in turn generates physical

82

disorders. The way in such cases to heal the body is not to treat the physical disorder, but to remove the sense of guilt and fear that has produced it.

I knew a young woman once who apparently was a perfectly healthy specimen. Yet she was paralyzed by fear. She was afraid to cross the street. She was afraid to meet people lest she contaminate them. She was afraid to be left alone with little children lest she harm them. She had lost the power to study and use her mind. She was helpless. But at the bottom of all this was a turgid, morbid sense of guilt. It had its beginnings in her childhood; it had grown until it had utterly mastered her and destroyed her ability to live in any normal fashion whatsoever. She was a helpless paralytic and she had lost all hope in herself and for herself. The doctors had assured her that physically nothing was the matter with her. And that was true. But when that load of guilt, that burden of self-accusation was removed; when that faulty reaction to life through fear was set straight, that moment her recovery began. Today she is a free and happy woman.

Thus, we may imagine that Jesus saw in this paralytic the spiritual disorder that had caused his physical helplessness. The boy himself may not have been aware of it. But Jesus was. Once the inner man had been restored, the body once more would begin to function. Once the burden had been removed which had lain upon heart and conscience, the rest would follow of itself. Jesus restored shaky limbs by putting new hope into a sin-fettered heart. When he said, "Thy sins be forgiven thee," then he had made it possible for him to rise and walk.

Here, then, we have plainly disclosed the sphere within which all those whose lives have been reinforced by the Spirit of Jesus may exercise the power of healing. It is too little understood, and it is far too seldom employed. There is a whole area, hitherto little explored but in our day discovered by medical research and inquiry, in which not only medical practitioners, not only those skilled in the theories of psychology, but laymen whose personalities have been surcharged with divine energies, may help to heal sufferers whose sufferings have been caused by a lack of harmony between the soul and God. The Church in our day should not be so immersed in other tasks as to overlook this divine mission of restoring the soul to peace and harmony and thus making it possible for paralyzed men and women to walk once more in joy and freedom. One recalls that great story of Pope Urban and Thomas

Aquinas. Thomas came to Rome to visit the Pope, who got up for him a gorgeous show. They stood together and watched it go by. "Thomas," said the Pope, "the Church can no longer say, 'Silver and gold have I none.'" "No," was the answer. "Neither can it say, 'Take up thy bed and walk.'" At the entrance of the Church of St. Anne de Beaupré one sees a pile of crutches, trusses, bandages, left there by those who had come to the famous shrine for healing. They had entered the church feeble and infirm. When they left it they were free and strong. The spiritual counterpart of that pile of impedimenta should be at the porch of every church. Can the Church do that? Can it do just that? If not, if it can perform no work of healing for those paralyzed by fear or sin or remorse or discouragement or sorrow, then of what use the Church with its buildings, its endowments, its organizations, its congregations and the rest? Upon its power to make men walk, the vindication of the Church must ultimately rest.

Come to the end of the story. It was plain from the looks on the faces of scribe and Pharisee that they were shocked at this presumption of Jesus in forgiving this man his sins. Yet the proof of his power and right to do just that was given to them without delay. " 'That you may know that the Son of Man has authority on earth to pardon sins'—He turned to the paralytic, and said, ... 'Rise, take up your mat and go home.' " [1] And he did. There was an argument that could not be denied. The man walked. All could see him walk. Of what use therefore to deny the power that made him walk?

Plenty of people still debate the Person of Jesus. Who and what was he? Wherein lies the difference between him and any other whose feet have trod this planet? The answer to this question is to be found not in the sphere of theory or speculation. It is to be found on the streets and in the homes and lives of men. The test of life lies in its capacity to produce life and in the quality of life which it produces. Because the Life that was in Jesus can make the blind to see, the lame to walk; can make the timid strong and those who are leprous and unclean good and pure, therefore we know that the Life that was in him was the very Life of God. Thus were the scribes and Pharisees answered in their day, and so are they answered in the day in which we live. For what Jesus did for the poor paralytic then, he has done for multitudes ever since. And he is doing it today.

[1] Weymouth translation.

"I say unto thee, Arise." That is what Jesus always says to the physically and morally infirm. It may seem impossible. Bound by habit, restriction, by circumstance, hindered by obstacles, deprived of advantage, defeated by disappointment, weakened by indulgence, the ability to arise to the higher levels of manhood is no longer there. But Jesus always appealed to the hidden powers. He knew what was *in* man; knew that beneath all the inhibitions, complexes, fears, and distrust of self, there lay unsuspected spiritual resources. Jesus, imbued with Life-giving power, stood over the man who seemed helpless and impotent and said, "Rise and walk."

That a truly revolutionary psychological principle is to be found here, is not open to doubt or even to question. Here lay the divine strategy of Jesus in his dealing with men. He assumed the existence in every man of this hidden capacity to rise from weakness into spiritual stature and strength. To it he made his appeal, putting behind it the full strength of his own personality. Thus were the infirm equipped with the necessary resources for instant and victorious action. Here is a spiritual phenomenon to be reckoned with as the world's greatest moral force.

Helpers of their fellow men will always imitate this method of Jesus in dealing with the morally infirm. Many people are looking for deliverance to-day from the moral ills that beset them. Beneath the mask of a happy exterior there are torn and frustrated, divided and defeated natures that are looking for some power which will release them from the evils in which they are caught. They come with all kinds of explanations and excuses. They plead the extenuations of difficulty both outward and inward. They seek to make reasons for moral defeat plausible and intelligible. They point out the impossibility for themselves of attaining ideal standards of life and conduct. How shall we deal with them?

The part of prudence might seem to be not to expect too much of such people; to make allowance and concessions; to expect only a part-way performance; to admit that the ideal is not possible of immediate attainment. As a matter of fact, such a procedure is a profound mistake. If the truth were known, it would bring actual if not acknowledged disappointment to the moral invalid himself. In his heart he hopes for a word of hope, of promise and of command. He wants to be held to what he himself knows is the ideal course of conduct and of life.

He wants inexorable requirement, with no concession to weakness. Actually, also, the one sure safe course to self-recovery is not its gradual but its immediate attainment; not getting at it by degrees, but at once. Within the man, however infirm, there do lie these powers of action, the slumbering will, the capacity to conquer difficulty, throw off habits of indulgence, and achieve a liberated manhood. Standards will not be lowered out of deference to weakness; they will be held rigid out of respect for strength. The man will be told that what is expected is the ideal of life and conduct, the achievement of which lies in his very grasp. "I say unto thee, Arise." The appeal, with the whole weight of influence behind it on the part of him who makes it, will work a spiritual miracle. The infirm will walk upright.

Precisely this was what happened in our story. Thus far the man on the bed had done nothing. His friends had brought him to Jesus. They had supplied the faith that was needed. Jesus had spoken the word of pardon and release. Now came the supreme moment. The man himself must act. The will must spring to life. His salvation was compacted in that one simple, glorious act of the will. In those few dramatic moments there was born in his heart the conviction that obedience to the call and command of Jesus would bring him liberation. And it did.

So far as I can see there is only one thing that can make persons of us, and that is contact with others who are persons already. We all know of people who exercise a powerful influence over us just by what they are. To be near them means for us a communication of strength and courage that makes our palsied natures whole again. The supreme example of this, in his dealing with men, is the Person of Jesus. Winifred Kirkland in her helpful book *As Far as I Can See* has written:

If I had no other reason for seeking to make [His] presence real beside me, it would be enough that the effect brings utter exhilaration of my entire personality. The effect is typical and mental as well as spiritual. I feel my shoulders squaring, my head lifting. I am conscious of an inflow of health through all my body. . . . . Thus in contact with the Man of Nazareth, imagined, visualized, realized, through all my petty matter-of-fact hours, I experience a liberating of all my being, body and brain and heart and soul.[2]

"The man rose, and immediately under the eyes of all took up his mat and went out, so that they

[2] Used by permission of the publishers, Charles Scribner's Sons.

were all filled with astonishment, gave glory to God, and said, 'We never saw anything like this.' " [3] So the story ended then. And so the story of many a man's liberation from the paralyzing effect of sin or sorrow or failure ends today. And when men see it they are filled with awe and they give glory to God for giving such power to men.

[3] Weymouth translation.

CHAPTER FIVE

"WHO TOUCHED ME?"

MATTHEW 9:20-22; MARK 5:25-34; LUKE 8:43-48

JESUS WAS ON HIS WAY TO THE HOME OF JAIRUS.
He was in haste, for Jairus' daughter lay at the point
of death.[1] But he proceeded with some difficulty
through the dense and gesticulating crowd. And
in this crowd was this poor woman who had been a
sufferer for many years. She had spent all that she
had on medical treatment, yet grew steadily worse.
She merits our special attention because of the
nature of her suffering. She was not a leper, she
was not blind. She was not a paralytic, she suffered
from no deadly disease. No; she was a victim of
chronic debility, nervous exhaustion, lingering and
increasing loss of physical vitality. In a word, she
is the type of sufferer to which so many thousands
of people in the world today belong. They are able
to move about, they are not deformed or helpless.
But within them there is this terrible sense of weakness, of absence of all mental or nervous energy.

[1] For the story of Jairus' daughter see Chapter IV in the author's
Religion and Life, Harper & Bros., 1935.

92

They are incapable of vigorous action of any kind. Their case is all the more pitiable because outwardly there seems to be nothing the matter with them. They often fail to receive the sympathy they deserve, because their friends feel that they might do better if they would only exert themselves. They are thus isolated creatures, left to one side, misunderstood even by members of their own families, yet craving a word, a touch, the communication of life and strength that would heal them and enable them to take their place in the world once more. They have consulted physicians, psychologists, psychiatrists, and have spent much money and are no better—rather worse. They have suffered sometimes under their hands, yet have endured the treatment in hope of finding a way out of this mental and nervous misery. To this company this poor woman belonged, and the story of her healing holds out hope to all who suffer as she did.

She had heard of Jesus and of his power to heal the sick. She felt, if only she could get to him that he might give her back her health. How little times have changed when we get down deep into the necessities of human living and the realities of human experience. Let a man come into any community today with a reputation for healing disease

93

and how quickly people will crowd around him. We have had illustrations in our day. Some years ago Mr. Coué came to us with his famous formula for keeping well. Later an Englishman, Mr. Hicks, came with his method of the prayer of faith for the healing of the sick. Halls and churches were crowded, and the sick were brought to them in the hope that they might be healed. It is easy to understand why this poor woman wanted to come to Jesus.

But she was timid. She did not have the courage to approach him openly and before all the people. And so, as he passed by, she came as near to him as she could, put out her hand, and touched the border of his garment; for she said, "If I may touch but his clothes I shall be whole."

It was her great need, then, that brought this woman to Jesus. Now, what suffering is in the world for is a great mystery. The problem of evil has always been our greatest problem. It is as old as Job and as fresh as yesterday. No complete or satisfying answer has ever been given to it. We try in vain to solve it. We may throw light upon it. We may discover some uses to which suffering may be put. But ultimately there is a problem which belongs to God and not to us. One thing we may know: suffering and pain do bring people to God

94

as nothing else. The story of this woman can be multiplied many times over. Let a person know what physical suffering is; let him enter that strange land of invalidism which people in health know nothing whatever about, and he is brought by this experience into a fellowship with God, into a nearness to Christ, who is "touched with the feeling of our infirmities," more intimate, more real than he has known before. The little trials—these may cause us to fume or even to blaspheme. But the great tragedies of life—these do bring us to God. A French writer has said: "The trials of life often make us accuse Heaven; but the great sorrows make us quiet, make us listen." If we have a need which no one else has been able to meet; a problem no one else has been able to solve; suffering no human hand has been able to assuage, let us do what this woman did—bring it to Christ; make it not a reason for forsaking him, but of coming as close to him as we can.

She came to him, but she came in an extraordinary fashion. She simply put out her hand and touched his garment. Why did she do that? The ordinary interpretation is that she had the superstitious notion, current in her day, about the healing virtues of the clothes of the prophets. Emblems of

95

the law or of the Temple worship were often embroidered on the robes of Jewish rabbis. Jesus may have been wearing such a garment, the gift of a beloved disciple. This ignorant woman may have thought that just to touch it, would give her the health that she sought. For all that she knew of him were these vague rumors of the miraculous powers which he possessed.

That may be the meaning of it. And if it is, a very beautiful lesson comes out of it: the way that Jesus is willing to accept just such a little crumb of faith. He took that dark and superstitious idea and he called it faith. He called it faith because it had desire behind it, because it had trust in it, and love too, a love that was sure that any contact with Jesus would be different from anything she had ever known. It is well to bear this lesson in mind in our dealings with men. We would hardly have called that act an act of faith. Imagine us dealing with one who had such an idea as that. Would we not say to her: "My dear woman, you must go away and get better, more intelligent, more spiritual ideas than that about Jesus before you can expect him to do anything for you. You must have more satisfying, more scriptural ideas of salvation before you can receive it for yourself." But Jesus himself did nothing of the kind. He called this faith and he rewarded it. He distinguished, as we so often fail to do, between desire and the way of expressing desire. It was her passionate, though ignorant, belief that he could cure her that counted with him. So he accepted her faith though it was like a grain of mustard seed. Faith, according to Jesus, is simply stretching out the hand for what he has to give.

It is well for us that Jesus was willing to accept this woman's faith, for how true it is that often we have little more to offer. It is true of all of us sometimes, and of some of us always, that we touch but the hem of his garment. Our contacts with him are occasional, intermittent. Our ideas about him are vague and sometimes even border on the superstitious. We want our marriage to be blessed in his name. We take our children to him for baptism. We look to him at the sacramental hour of death. Birth, marriage, death—these throughout the ages have been connected with religion. At certain hours of need we are drawn to him. Yet who knows how much of ignorance may be lurking in our faith? How feeble that faith often is. And even the saintliest among us touch only the fringe of the Life that was in him. Yet if he accepted that woman's faith, he will accept ours, however ignorant it may be, if only desire, trust, love be at the heart of it.

Yet it is quite possible that the faith of this woman was not so ignorant and superstitious after all. Even with the words retained, "If I may touch but his clothes, I shall be whole," another interpretation is possible. And it is noticeable that Luke the physician in his account omits those words. Did he have a deeper insight? Did he see more clearly into this poor woman's heart? She had intended to stop Jesus and make her appeal. She would fall at his feet, make him notice her as she knelt there and implore him to have mercy on her and heal her. So had she planned it. And then, at the supreme moment, her courage had failed her. The reticence and reserve of her oriental womanhood asserted itself and held her back. And in agony, as he was about to pass, in a swift, involuntary gesture which may have had in it even the despairing instinct to stop and detain him, she put out her hand, hardly knowing what she did, and touched but the hem of his garment as Jesus passed by.

"Who touched me?" Jesus had paused at once, and turned around. The disciples, hearing the question, answered just as we would have answered: "You see the crowd pressing you on all sides, and

yet you ask 'Who touched me?'" Some have said
that unconsciously she must have gripped his clothes
or even tugged at them nervously to make him
notice her. But that does justice neither to the
woman nor to Jesus. And such an idea gives no
meaning to the later word of Jesus that he realized
at her touch that healing power had gone from him.
No, hers was but a timid touch, and yet he knew.
Some may have touched him unavoidably: others out
of curiosity or from conventional courtesy or ordinary reverence. But when, out of all this company,
one individual isolated herself and, however timidly,
touched but his garment from deep controlling desire and passionate belief, then his whole personality
responded instantly. That touch differentiated itself so subtly, so sharply, from all other forms of
contact that he stopped and asked: "Who touched
my clothes?"

Such was the sensitiveness of Jesus to human need.
Such was his instant response to moral and spiritual
appeal. It was, and is, impossible for anyone to
need him without his knowledge. There was in
him this inward divination of spiritual want and
desire. No one can touch him as this woman did
without his swift awareness of it. That sensitiveness
to need is an indispensable characteristic of all the

helpers of men. There are men and women in the world, as we all know, who have almost uncanny ways of perceiving another's need. They are sensitive to the slightest word, the most timid approach. There comes the instant response, the complete understanding, the overflowing sympathy that blesses and that cures. Such natures perform a great healing ministry as they pass along the daily pathway of their lives. It makes us ask ourselves how many people may be coming in contact with us day by day with all kinds of secret needs, putting forth, it may be, a timid hand in the hope that we will notice them, turn and help them? Yet we are not aware that anyone has touched us at all. Perhaps one of our deepest prayers should be that we should have something of this inward sensitiveness to need that shall make us quickly aware of it and cause us to turn to it as surely, as infallibly, as the needle to the pole.

Now Jesus, as we have seen, was in haste. Jairus' daughter was at the point of death. And this woman was but a chronic sufferer in no immediate danger. She had survived her suffering for twelve years, might survive it for twelve years more. But Jesus would not pass this woman by. For him no mission was so important, no task so imperative that it war-

100

ranted the neglect of the immediate need that presented itself to him. He did not hurry on in order to reach a moment sooner the bedside of the daughter of Jairus.

How much we need to imitate this method of Jesus in our daily life and work. We too are in haste. Some important task awaits us. We have no time to spare. And thus we are absent-minded as we pass hurriedly on our way. The scholar, the preacher, the businessman, are all absorbed in their intensive thinking. They meet their best friends in the street, seem to look them in the eye and pass them with no sign of recognition. Even suffering which at another time they would gladly relieve passes unnoticed. They are absent-minded because their minds are absent from men and their needs. Jesus was never so absorbed in what he had in mind to do that he overlooked the deed that needed to be done as he passed by.

But let us come back to the faith of this woman. Jesus can do nothing without faith. And if the faith of this woman was not the superstitious notion that if she but touched his garment she would in some miraculous manner be healed, of what was it then compounded? What were its ingredients? First of all, there was her deep desire to be healed.

101

Then there was her glorious conviction that Jesus, because of what she knew he was, could make her whole. That was her faith, her desire, and her intense expectancy. These had been the creative agents of her cure. It was not her mere act which effected the result, but the thought and emotion which inspired and accompanied it. And that is faith.

The story shows us all what a simple thing faith really is. We make it far too difficult. How often we hear people say that they lack faith; or that they wished that they had more faith; or that they do not know whether they have any faith or not. They make it all too obscure, too intellectual, as if it involved believing this or that which they feel they do not or cannot believe.

Now it is a good thing, and I am not saying a word in disparagement of it, to have a good working theology, to be well grounded in one's opinions. But behind all that there is just this one question: Do we want to be a different man or woman physically, morally, or spiritually from what we feel ourselves to be? It is perfectly possible, that is, for a person to be orthodox, complacent, to have all kinds of evangelical and scriptural ideas, without having the remotest desire or intention of being a different

102

or a better man next week than he is today. And we can imagine on the other hand people down in Central Africa or the South Sea Islands, let us say, lacking education in Christian ideas or even knowledge of them, and yet behind all that having a real moral desire and a deep moral willingness to be made different by the touch of Jesus Christ. And of the first, we must say that they lack faith in the New Testament sense of it; and of the second, that they possess it.

The root question in religion is, Do we desire to be different from what we feel ourselves to be; and are we willing to be changed into something better by the touch of Jesus? Are we wishing to have his presence, his power, his salvation in our lives? The root things in religion are always the same things, and they are always simple things. The ways of getting at them are different, that is all. The Roman Catholic gets at them in one way, the Protestant in another; the mystic, the rationalist, the practical man, each has his way of getting at them. And I do not say that one way is as good as another. Yet I do say that the way we get at them is not the crucial or the decisive thing. It is this: Do we wish to approach Jesus at all with the desire and expectation of being changed into a different man or wom-

103

an? Do we want to be different, and do we believe that he can make us better than we feel ourselves to be? If so, then we have faith. It may not be a perfect faith. This woman's was not. At best it was incomplete and uninformed. It is not perfect faith but a perfect Saviour that heals us. We should never shrink back because we do not know enough or believe enough. To be conscious of our need, to believe that he can give us what we need, that is the essence of faith that heals and saves. Teachers and preachers of religion can perform no higher service for those whom they seek to help than to make clear what faith really is.

We come to the conclusion of the story. The woman was healed by her touch of him, but Jesus did not leave her until he had established some personal connection between her and himself. He paused. He was at once conscious that some healing virtue had passed from him. That touch of faith was sufficient to release the spiritual power and energy that was in him. And that sudden access of power accomplished the woman's cure. Modern medical science would not call that a miracle today, because the power of personality to effect cures without the use of material means is now well understood. The fact of such cures is no longer ques-

104

tioned, nor is its method any longer open to doubt. It lies within the power of a personality surcharged with the energies of life, to transmit that energy into the sufferer and thereby bring about his cure. It is a high calling and it makes high demands upon him who exercises it. No one ever works cures like this without himself being conscious that virtue has passed out of him.

But why did Jesus pause, the woman being already healed? Why could he not leave the timid woman to shrink back into obscurity? She was now perfectly well. Why bring her out into the center of that scene and expose her to the open and curious scrutiny of the crowd? It must have cost that shrinking woman more than we can conceive to come trembling and fall down at his feet and tell him all the truth, declare before all the people for what cause she had touched him and how she was healed. Yet Jesus could not let her go until he knew that her healing was complete, nor until she knew how her healing had been wrought. She must not go away with body healed, but spirit still infirm. She must not pass forever from his sight with any darkened or ignorant ideas of how she had been healed. Jesus could not let it go like that. He must establish the personal relationship. And so he asked the question, "Who touched me?" and looked around to see who had done it. And when the woman saw that she could conceal herself no longer, she came in fear and trembling and fell down before him, and before all the people, in plain sight of everyone. Surely there was an act of courage, an act of love, which revealed the true nature of the woman, her earnestness, her gratitude, her utter devotion to him who had answered her prayer. She had touched him again, but this time not his clothes but his heart. And then Jesus called her by a name. He called her "My daughter." And we can hear the voice of tenderness and of love with which he spoke the words. "My daughter, thy faith hath made thee whole, body and soul. Now go in peace." And when she went away, she went not only with a healed body, but with peace and joy in her heart. She had the idea of a new Friend, a new Master, a new Saviour whom she loved and who loved her. She went home the possessor and the bearer of a true and living faith.

We know nothing of her future. She returned to her home as he had bidden. But she never forgot. And one thing she surely did. She shared her experience with others: "He hath made me whole." The relationship which Jesus had established between him and her grew and deepened and expanded until it reached all the sympathies and interests of her life. Truly she had been made whole.

I lay the story down and I find that the final impression left on me is not so much the woman's faith in Jesus, as Jesus' faith in her. The great power of the Lord is that he comes to human life with faith. We talk of the difficulty of believing in him. But we think too little of his still greater difficulty in believing in us. Yet he does. He believed that that poor woman had the capacity within her to receive, to understand, to appropriate, and to use the gift of God which he gave her. He believes in us, even the weakest and the worst. Our faith in him depends upon his faith in us. Jesus always believed in the possibility of men turning and repenting and rising into their full stature as the children of God. All true helpers of men have this invincible faith in them. G. K. Chesterton has said of St. Francis that he treated the whole mob of men as if they were a lot of kings. To have power over men like the power of Jesus, it is necessary to share Jesus' everlasting faith in the least and lowliest of the children of God.

CHAPTER SIX

THE POOL OF BETHESDA

JOHN 5:1-9

THIS PASSAGE RECORDS ONE OF THE MOST touching and suggestive narratives to be found in the Gospels. There was a feast of the Jews and Jerusalem was crowded. In and about the city in Jesus' day were several natural springs which appear to have possessed healing virtues for certain ailments. The most famous of these was known as the Pool of Bethesda, which recent exploration has located at the northwest corner of the Temple enclosure. It was an intermittent mineral spring where waters bubbled up from time to time. The people superstitiously ascribed this to the action of supernatural beings, so that the healing powers of the Bethesda waters were felt to be due to an "angel" who "troubled the waters." There must have been cures; so only can we account for the reputation of the place. Otherwise the crowd would not have continued to come year after year, just as today it keeps coming to Lourdes. We touch here a psychological phenomenon which it is not my purpose to explore.

To this pool, then, Jesus found his way on the Sabbath of the Feast of the Tabernacles, and what a picture it presented to his eyes. About it, on all sides, lay sick folk, blind, lame, diseased, waiting with strained eyes, watching the water in frenzied anxiety, their friends eager to help them. Then the mad rush when the moment came! One first—and for the rest the miserable return to waiting again. Ah! In those porches there were as many broken hearts as there were broken bodies. It requires no gift of imagination to understand how the heart of Jesus was wrung with the misery and the pathos of it all. And see what he instinctively did. His eye roamed over the whole crowd until it singled out this one most hopeless case, precisely as the trained eye of the surgeon quickly selects the worst case in the waiting room. Jesus always distinguished the individual from the mass. He detached one man, one woman from the multitude and let the full power of his personality fall upon him. It was Jesus' way of dealing with men—not in the aggregate but in the concrete. And it should be ours.

"When Jesus saw him lie." It did not take Jesus long to select his man. There was something about the way he lay there that differentiated him from all the rest—an aspect of helplessness and hopelessness. And with practiced eye Jesus "knew that he had now been a long time in that case." Thirty-eight years—a helpless invalid for thirty-eight years. Yet that was not the most pitiful part of it all. This came out a moment later after Jesus had spoken to the man. "Sir, I have no man, when the water is troubled, to put me into the pool." Behind every other sufferer there was a friend to help him get down into the water. But this man was friendless. Day after day he had sat there helpless, his eyes watching to see when the water would bubble, edging himself nearer and nearer. And every time doomed to disappointment. Before he could work his poor infirm body down to the water, somebody else with quick, strong friendly arms behind him would get there first and the poor man would have to crawl back and wait again. It must have been the hopelessness in his face more than the helplessness of his body that attracted the attention of Jesus. There was an expression of vacancy, an emptiness of despair that made its instant appeal; so, when Jesus saw him lying there like that he singled him out from all the rest.

In the words, "I have no man," we find the cruelty of that scene. It was not a scene of absolute inhumanity. Indeed, there was much that was beau-

110

tiful about it. There was plenty of helpfulness there, love, sympathy; and pity in abundance. Men were engaged in helping others, anxious about their own sick, eagerly doing everything to bring health and healing to those whom they loved. What a scene of compassion it was. Yet there was not one single soul in the whole picture who had a hand or a heart or a thought for this poor friendless man who made his frantic futile effort and took his bitter disappointment year after year and patiently waited only to lose out again and again. No one ever noticed that dull, mute look of despair. Each helper was so busy taking care of his own friend that he did not even see this lonely, helpless man.

But the man whom no one else saw was the one man whom Jesus saw. The one whom all the rest neglected was the very man whom Jesus chose. That was Jesus. And that is the religion of Jesus. To love the unloved, to love the loveless, to befriend the friendless—this is to imitate the method of Jesus in his dealing with men. When Jesus entered the scene of pitiful need at the Pool of Bethesda, a revolution was wrought in the moral history of mankind. Nowhere on earth today where his name is known, could that scene repeat itself. A poor helpless man could not say today, "I have no man." I returned lately from a state hospital for the mentally infirm. I found myself in a room filled with derelicts, an unimaginable company of destitute, defective human beings. Judged by any other standards than those of Jesus, they were worthless fragments of humanity. Yet behind every one of them were nurses, internes, and skilled physicians giving them all the care that knowledge and sympathy can bring. Our Pools of Bethesda are different places from what they were in Jesus' day, because of what he did there so long ago.

Every one of us can test the quality of his sympathy by asking himself whom am I helping? Every one of us is helping his friends. Our solicitude for those whom we love is quick, instinctive, limitless. There is nothing we will not do for them. But it is only when with the eyes of Jesus we detect one who, but for us, would have no man to help him, and put ourselves behind him until his rescue and healing have been achieved, that we are imitating the method of Jesus in his dealing with men. In a too little known novel by Lily Dougall written years ago, entitled *Beggars All,* occurs this sentence: "If each well-to-do person would help along one poor one, there would be no 'masses.' . . . . The multitudes

112

belong to God; the one or two I can give part of my life for, he has given to me."

Well, here lay the man who had been thirty-eight years in such a case. John gives us these exact details in his Gospel. He had doubtless been at pains to verify them. He may have gone to the man afterward and asked him. But he does not tell us what was the matter with him. The common idea has been that he was a cripple. But this is not in the text. We are told only that he had an infirmity for thirty-eight years. The point emphasized is that his was apparently an incurable disease. He was a hopeless case. And we are reminded at this point that for Jesus there are no hopeless cases. A first question often asked of a sick person today is, "How long have you been in this case?" And if the answer is, "For a long time," the practitioner will often shake his head and say, "I am sorry, but I can do nothing for you." But Jesus would take anyone on. He did not distinguish between cases that were seemingly capable of being cured and those that were not. A man who had had an infirmity for thirty-eight years is a symbol of one who from every human point of view is incurable. But for Jesus there were no incurables. It was a matter of immense moment and importance in Jesus' dealing with men then, and it

113

is in his dealing with men today. Often men will say of themselves that there is no hope. They have been so long in such a case. Ingrained habit cannot be overcome, acquired instincts cannot be eradicated. Their characters have settled in definite molds which cannot be altered. For them the day of reformation has passed. What they are, that they must continue to be. Whether it be sensual habit or what people are pleased to call their temperament, these are fixed. But as Jesus confronted the man who had been infirm for thirty-eight years, so he confronts men today, no matter how long they have been "in such a case," with his word of promise and of hope.[1]

Helpers of men would do well to imitate this strategy of Jesus in dealing with men. No matter what the infirmity may be, physical, moral, or mental, and no matter how long men may have been in such a case, always they will be confronted with this attitude of hope and command. Even in all kinds of physical infirmity, the belief on the part of the sufferer that he can get well is a major factor in his getting well. The way of faith is the way to health. If the sufferer says that he has been told on competent medical authority that his is an incurable case, it will

---

[1] "Jesus was the great psychotherapist of his day. He loved to stand before man and say, 'Wilt thou be made whole?'"—*H. E. Fosdick.*

be well to remind him that there are no incurable diseases. Diseases are called incurable because physicians have not yet found the means of curing them. More than one patient has recovered—to the astonishment of his doctor—who has persistently cultivated the indomitable hope of recovery and has fought disease by the operation of a courageous will. Similarly with respect to long, ingrained habits in immoral living. Let the will which lies like a sleeping giant within the subconscious self be suddenly and sufficiently aroused, and it will throw off the shackles of apparently invincible habit and the man will become free. The therapeutic value of what is popularly known as "conversion" has long been recognized by physicians and psychologists, and the evidence of its power to accomplish seemingly impossible results is overwhelming and convincing.

So, also, with respect to what we call our moods or our temperament. To a great many people, what they call temperament is a finality. They would like to be cheerful and not morose. They admire people who can always be courteous and controlled, whereas they are short and snappy; who can be steadily industrious, whereas they can work only in jerks or spasms. But of course, with their temperament, this cannot be expected of them. There are

115

plenty of people all around us who have long ago surrendered any idea of getting over their long-standing infirmities or, if the truth were known, any desire to do so. But the wise counselor will waste no pity on them at all. Slavery to temperament, they will be reminded, is as ignoble as surrender to any other form of tyranny. They will be told that the force of old established and pernicious habits of mind has been much overestimated; their conquest is by no means the almost impossible feat that it is generally considered to be; that there is danger that we make the pathway to self-recovery difficult by representing it to be impossible; that the road to manhood lies in keeping the will operating vigorously; that our temperaments are intended to be the servants and not the masters of our wills.

Thus did Jesus meet the case of this man who had been an invalid for thirty-eight years. He came to him with a peremptory challenge which penetrated at once to the man's inmost nature, which pierced beyond his physical infirmity to the one possible obstacle to his cure. He asked him the direct question, "Wilt thou be made whole?" It must have startled the man. What a strange and apparently unfeeling question to have asked of one who for so long had haunted this place of healing. Why had he been there all these years if he had not wanted to get well? Yet Jesus well knew that a man may have a sick soul as well as a sick body. Sometimes protracted invalidism does damage to a man's morals. It may produce self-pity, one of the most dangerous of moral maladies. It may even tempt people to protract their invalidism when they might rise above it. They may get so accustomed to the invalid life of inactivity that they are not really eager for the responsibilities and labor that are expected of the robust. They may become so used to having other people wait on them that they are not keen on taking care of themselves. All of these moral dangers and more threaten the chronic invalid. And doctors and nurses are well aware of it.

Did the man really want to get well, and go about Jerusalem and get a job and be self-supporting and cease to be an object of charity? Or was he will-ridden as well as bedridden? Jesus could do nothing for others unless and until he was assured that the will was on his side. The one thing which he required was desire and a co-operating will. It was his uniform demand. Everything was possible with that one imperative moral requisite; and nothing without it. Desire backed by will—this, according to Jesus, is the faith that saves; willingness to make the

117

great effort in the belief that it will accomplish the desired result. It may be an imperfect faith. But it must be a believing faith. And it must be an active co-operating faith.

There are many people who are troubled by the fact that even though they have a creed, nothing seems to happen. Of course nothing happens. Faith is not a passive thing, a magic key. Faith is a vital force; it is a passionate, co-operating act of the will. We find that note in the Gospels about faith on the part of all sufferers whom Jesus healed. They did not have a finished faith, but they wanted desperately to be healed, and they trusted that Jesus could give them the healing they desired. That was all.

Well, that was the problem that was presented to Jesus. Could he have this co-operating faith in the heart of this man who had suffered from his infirmity for thirty-eight years? Day after day, year after year, he had come up there until the hope or even the desire to get well may have left him. There he was, disappointed, heartsick, helpless, hopeless. And that mood was the most difficult obstruction to the faith that Jesus needed in every sufferer that he cured. And it is today. Long experience of disappointments, the well-remembered disillusionments and

118

failures; the acceptance at last of the condition in which we find ourselves; the lack of expectation that we can ever be any different—this is the obstacle which must be removed, the difficulty that must be overcome. Such is the inner meaning of the question asked by Jesus. Do you still have the desire to be well? Will you trust me and co-operate with me that you may become whole? It was, as I have said, a challenge. It penetrated beneath the veneer of the man's bitterness of heart. It summoned him to one more effort. And the man answered that question. He met that challenge. "Lord, I have struggled to get well." And he told a pitiful story of past disappointments to prove to Jesus how much he wanted to be healed. "I have had no man." But he had one at last. He had the very man he needed. He had the man Jesus. And Jesus did not wait for the stirring of the waters. All that he waited for was the stirring of the will.

The whole significance of Jesus for human experience, absolutely all of it, lies in enabling men and women to do the one thing that they say they cannot do. To take up his bed and walk it was the one thing this poor infirm man could not do. And he did it. Jesus always begins when human strength

119

ends. Precisely at the point where life gets beyond us, he proposes to take it over.

The same inexorable requirement will be made by every true helper of men today. There is no point in dealing with people on any other level. All excuses, palliations, appeals for a pitying extenuation of the moral invalid because of repeated and futile efforts at self-recovery, because of weaknesses and lack of inner resources, will be swept aside. Underneath them all, it will be understood, is this terrible inertia, this unwillingness to rise in hope and faith. "Wilt thou be made whole?" Are you willing to pay the price, say good-by to old and loved indulgences, break with your past? Do you really want to get over your moral weakness, or are you in your heart still clinging to it? Is there something within you that does not want to be stirred? What is needed always and everywhere is this summons to action. When Jesus came into the porches by the quiet waters of *waiting*, he came with a message of *action*. Thus he dealt with the man who had been so long "in such a case." So we will deal with him also.

And then came the peremptory word of command: "Get up, take up your mat, and walk." The words are staccato, every one of one syllable. Their impact, with the personality of Jesus behind them, on the will of the man was instant and decisive. The angel troubled the water but Jesus stirred the springs of the man's soul. That was the critical moment for the man. Had he hesitated, had he waited, there would have been no healing for him. The immediate response of his will was the way to his salvation. He rose and walked for the first time in thirty-eight years.

The same truth holds today. In dealing with all impotent folk, the first necessity is to make sure of deep underlying desire, of a will ready to co-operate. Assured of this, one will then make this quick, sharp appeal to instant action. You say you cannot do this or that. You can. Now do it in defiance of all seeming impossibility. "Take up your bed and walk." Act at once. The little word "Now" is the gateway into healing and life. That Kingdom is captured only by will and action. The first impulse must be obeyed. In the heart of the most infirm, of those who have been longest "in such a case," there are inner resources which need only immediate obedience to direct appeal to be brought into operation and to work a moral revolution. Just this or that impulse once obeyed can convert the downward into the upward trend of life. Immediately the ef-

121

fort is made, the infirm person finds that he *can* walk. The inner resolve, the courageous response, brings the divine power. Thus may one make contact with undreamed-of energies. Miracles are the surprises of those who have sufficient courage to make them their own.

"Take up your bed." The man was to roll up the mattress which he had used for so long. He must not leave it spread out in case he should be tempted to lie back on it again. He must absolutely discard what had been the symbol of his weakness for all those years. He must put away the wretched thing because never would he need it or use it again. He must burn his bridges behind him. Again, this word of Jesus finds its immediate application in the treatment of infirm people today. Not one miserable excuse must be left for them to fall back on. There must be an act so definite, so clean-cut, that one is absolutely committed to the new course of action, so that going back is impossible. And the man was to *walk!*

A man who had been on his back for thirty-eight years might be expected to grope and stagger around a bit. But Jesus had nothing of that sort in mind. He seemed to expect immediate spiritual robustness. Men were to step right out and begin at once and not by degrees the exacting careers of the completely fit. No limping, no looking around for someone to hold you up and keep you going. No just managing to get about. On your feet, moving with vigor and despatch. Spiritual invalidism can end instantly, or the gospel of Jesus is not what ten thousand times ten thousand have found it to be.[2]

The story does not end there. The stories of Jesus' healings never end there. They do not end with what happened to men's bodies. Jesus was not willing to leave it like that. He was not willing to leave the man like that. So there is a sequel to the story. It seems that the man was well known to the Jewish officials. He was a familiar spectacle. So, instead of marveling over his miraculous cure, when they saw him walking about freely, they pointed out to him that he had no right to be carrying his mattress on a feast day. Even this was an infringement of the sabbatical law as interpreted by traditionalism. The man's reply was direct and honest. "The man who healed me told me to take up my mattress and walk." And they asked him, "Who told you to do this?" The man said that he did not know. For Jesus had passed out unnoticed, there being a crowd in the place where the man was healed. But later

[2] From a sermon by Henry Sloane Coffin, reported in the *Christian World Pulpit*, August 20, 1925. Used by permission of Dr. Coffin.

123

Jesus found him in the Temple area. He was not through with the man yet. He was well of body, but so long as his inner life was not pure and strong, the man was not truly restored to health. What Jesus then said to him completed the inward healing. "See, your body is well and strong. Now leave off all sinful habits lest something worse happen to you." The natural inference of these words is that the man's disease had been brought on by sinful living. Lifelong misery may be caused by one's earliest moral failures. Another implication of this word of Jesus, also verified by all our knowledge of pathology, is that even the years of suffering endured by this man had not of necessity broken the power of those sinful habits. He knew why he was diseased and shattered. Yet even in those first days of restored health there lay the danger of returning to the old way of living. Over and over again it has been proved that no amount of suffering of itself purifies from sin. The man had another effort of the will to make. As he had risen from the bed of his physical infirmity, so he must rise above the power of sin over his life. As he had trusted and obeyed Jesus in the outward cure, so let him now inwardly and morally obey. Thus, as always, Jesus looked beyond the external to the internal, through the

124

physical to the spiritual. No man is in health, teaches Jesus, until he has a healthy soul.

The future of this man is shrouded in some obscurity. "The man departed, and told the Jews that it was Jesus, which had made him whole." Now, why did he do that? Was it thoughtless? Did he think they had a right to know? Had he no idea that this would involve Jesus in the difficulties which, as the sequel shows, actually befell him as a result of the man's irresponsible act? Is it even credible that this man was a backslider and, once restored to physical health, gave little heed to future consequences either to himself or to Jesus? For myself, I prefer to believe that the man rose to the higher levels of manhood in response to the word of Jesus that he break with his past, with his old life, with his old habits, and, filled with new-born gratitude and hope, went and boldly told the Jews, told everyone, what great things had been done for him by the man Jesus.

The correlation of body and mind is one of the commonplaces of modern medicine. It is understood today that the mind has an immense influence over the body; and that bodily conditions have an effect on the state of one's mental and moral life.

Thus the professions of the ministry and of medicine overlap in our day. The doctor looks to the minister to give the patient the spiritual reinforcement which he needs; and the minister with a difficult case of a disordered personality consults the doctor to discover the physical cause of spiritual dislocation. The two today work hand in hand. This is in precise imitation of the method of Jesus in dealing with men. He drew no line between a man's body and his soul. The two together make up the man. And he is not the man he ought to be until both are strong and well.

It is a great mistake for those who seek by moral means to bring about the cure of suffering souls to work independently of medical science. There is a considerable amount of unwise amateur psychotherapy in our day that never achieves any permanent results. The first thing that a wise spiritual counselor will do if he seeks to treat a diseased personality, is to have the patient consult a competent physician to see if there be underlying physical causes for his mental and moral disease. Conversely, it must be admitted that medical science, or a purely secular psychiatry, often fails of itself to bring about the cure of a disordered life. A deeper remedy is needed. The springs of the soul must be reached and touched. This the wisest practitioners themselves are ready to admit. There exist any number of books on moral pathology that give an accurate analysis of moral disease. But one will page them all through in vain for counsel as to how anyone who is held in bondage to moral disease can be brought to moral life again. One such treatise has the engaging title, *The Service of Man,* but here is a quotation from it: "It is no use disguising the fact that there is no remedy for a bad heart." No remedy for a bad heart! Well, then, there are a lot of incurable people in the world. But it was precisely the heart of this impotent man that Jesus remedied before he left him. And that has been the glory of Christian healing ever since. "Give me," so runs an early Christian document, "one who is covetous and stingy, and I will hand him back to you generous and open-handed. Give me one who is afraid of death; he shall shortly despise crosses and fires and the torture. Give me one who is lustful and a glutton; you shall soon see him chaste and temperate." The power of inward cleansing, the power to create a new heart—this is the property of the Christian Evangel derived directly from Jesus, who swayed men's wills so that they achieved not only the conquest of physical ills, but of moral defect that lies at

127

the root of all forms of human disorder. When Jesus told the man who had been healed as to his body to leave off sins that could make him worse off than he was before, he was uttering a profound truth that lies at the center of the wisest treatment of impotent people today.

CHAPTER SEVEN

THE SYROPHOENICIAN WOMAN

MATTHEW 15:21-28; MARK 7:24-30

NEARLY ALL OF THE STORIES TO BE FOUND ON the pages of the Gospels about Jesus' dealing with men are easy to understand. There is no difficulty. They are simple, straightforward, direct, and contain nothing of doubtful interpretation. But this story is not so easy. We find things in it which give us pause. What did Jesus mean by saying that he was sent only to the lost sheep of the house of Israel? And why did he address this poor suppliant woman with words so seemingly harsh that it is with a feeling of pain that one reads them after nineteen hundred years? It must receive our very careful attention if it is to be understood.

Jesus, we read, withdrew from thence and went away into the parts of Tyre and Sidon, outside the Holy Land, away from Judea and from Galilee. It was Jesus' only trip abroad. And that was such a little one. For Tyre and Sidon are only a few miles above the frontier of Galilee on the seacoast. Still, this was the farthest that Jesus ever went from home.

How small was the area within which the whole short life of Jesus was spent! Yet what could miles have added to the breadth of his life? What needed he of more territory? How could he have lived a larger life by covering more ground? He lived all the life there was. The world in which he lived was as broad as the universe. It was bounded only by infinity. We are reminded that one cannot measure the breadth of a man's life today by his mileage, or by looking at the speedometer to see how far he has driven his car. Acreage does not tell the story. One's life is as broad as he is and no broader. Some people spend their time traveling round the world, and remain provincial to the core. Other people live in a restricted space, like the Brontë sisters, yet, in the words of Madame Guyon,

> These prison walls cannot control
> The flight, the freedom of the soul.

Why did Jesus withdraw from thence? He had been in Jerusalem, in debate with scribe and Pharisee. They had been talking about tradition; about the minutiae of ecclesiastical law. They had been asking Jesus why his disciples did not wash their hands in the manner prescribed, before they ate bread. Jesus wanted to get away from all that. He

130

was wearied with this insistence on ecclesiastical conformity and orthodoxy, with a formality which was far removed from his own religion of the spirit. And so he went away as far as Tyre and Sidon. And there, in heathendom, he found what he had failed to find in Jerusalem. He found in a poor Gentile woman what he had not found in the hearts of his own chosen people. Far from the center and citadel of institutional religion he found the faith that saves. And it might be true today that Jesus would walk away from some churches whose congregations had mistaken the rites and the formulas, the rules and the observances of religion for religion itself, and find the faith for which he waits in someone whom the orthodox would call a heathen.

When Jesus went away into Tyre and Sidon he crossed more than national frontiers. He crossed the line between the chosen race and "the lesser breeds," between elect and nonelect, between clean and unclean. He did a sensational and an unprecedented thing. He proclaimed in effect that his gospel was as broad as humanity; that it knew no restrictions. He overlooked completely the lines that men drew. He drew no lines; or, rather, the lines which he drew were vertical and not horizontal—between right and wrong; between sin and righteousness; between

life and death. In this story Jesus blessed with his
blessing an unholy race. The disciples were taught
a lesson which they never forgot. Here The Acts
of the Apostles were already written by the Spirit of
the Master. He laid very simply and naturally the
foundations of what we call world missions. Jesus
was himself the first foreign missionary. The gospel was not for some but for all. The good news
which he came to proclaim was "for all people." In
the simplicity of this story we find the authentica-
tion of the Christian program of carrying the gospel
to other lands.

When he came "into the borders of Tyre and
Sidon," as Mark tells us, he "entered into an house,
and would have no man know it: but he could not
be hid." Even into those regions the report of him
had come. People had heard of how he had healed
men of their sickness and suffering. These know no
frontiers. Suffering is one of those universal and
sacramental facts that bind the whole world together
in a comprehending unity. This story is as fresh
today as it was two thousand years ago. Everywhere
there is desire for deliverance from suffering: for
oneself, for those whom one loves. Logic and theory
have nothing to do with it. People leap over all

such barriers in their agonizing desire for healing and health.

So it was in Jesus' day. "Straightway a woman." It did not take long. "A Canaanitish woman whose little daughter had an unclean spirit." I suppose we would call it epilepsy. Mark adds a few details. She was a Syrophoenician woman, a Greek by birth or creed or both. She belonged to an alien and, to the Jews, an accursed race. And she had no one to plead her cause. She was alone and helpless in her need. It was not for herself, but for her daughter. A mother for her daughter. And she fell at his feet and begged him to drive the demon out of her little daughter. "Have mercy on me, O Lord, thou son of David." That was all she knew about him. She gave him all the title of respect at her command.

It was a distressing case. And Jesus needed rest and quiet. Here was an interruption, an intrusion, an impertinence. So it seemed to the disciples, who urged him to send her away, "For she crieth after us." I do not blame those disciples overmuch. I am wondering if we would not have done just that. We resent the sudden and unwelcome projection of the disagreeable into our lives. The sight of a destitute and diseased person is an offense. Instinctively we turn aside from it, seek to avoid it. It is not our affair. It lies outside the sphere of our duty. It upsets us. It interrupts our purpose and plans. We get away from it as rapidly as we can. By contrast, I note the attitude and method of Jesus. Nothing that was human failed to make its instant appeal. A case of human need was never an interruption. It made its immediate claim on time and strength. If human necessity lay in his path, he paused. He could not get beyond it. In this the example of Jesus is a standing reproach, a constant inspiration to us all.

So he stopped. And then there followed the extraordinary interview between Jesus and this poor woman pleading for her child. How strange and even harsh the attitude of Jesus seems to be. It is this that makes the story difficult for us. First we read that he answered her not a word. Then he told her that he was sent only to the lost sheep of the house of Israel. And finally he told her that it is not meet to take the children's bread and cast it to the dogs—and that sounds like a cruel insult to this suffering soul. How can we understand it?

It has been suggested that Jesus deliberately assumed an unsympathetic attitude in order to make a shining example of her. It pained her and it pained

134

him. "How it must have wrung his heart to treat her in a way so foreign to every fiber of his soul! But had he not so dealt with her, what a loss" to the world.[1] He repulsed her over and over again, treated her with what must have seemed to her as unaccountable and inexcusable harshness so as to show how much punishment she could take, and still rise superior to it. For myself, I cannot believe it. The idea is repugnant. I do not think that Jesus ever dealt with men like that. There remains the possibility that there was really no harshness at all, that it was all tenderness, and that the woman, with a woman's subtle divination, understood the tenderness that was in it all.

"He answered her not a word." That was not from lack of sympathy but from excess of it. There are times when we are speechless. Human need seems to be so far beyond anything that we can say. Instinctive reverence before acute suffering demands silence. Words seem an impertinence. So Jesus looked down on this woman, with her piteous plea for her daughter, with a heart so full of compassion that his lips did not move. There is something unspeakably eloquent in this silence of Jesus. It tells how deeply he was moved.

[1] "The Expositor's Bible," *St. Matthew, in loco.*

But he must have faith. As we read over carefully the stories of how Jesus helped men, we discover how he could not come to their aid unless they had at least a grain of faith. Over and over again he asked, "Believest thou?" There must be behind the plea for help some faith in his person, some spiritual bond between the suppliant and himself. So, before he could help this woman he must know that beneath her desire for her child there was some living, operating faith in him. Thus, he tested her to see if the faith were there. Although it seemed as if for a time he were refusing her plea, raising all kinds of objections and difficulties, yet all the while he was hoping that she would rise above them, encouraging her, too, that she might have the marvelous blessing which she sought.

It is a familiar device with all wise helpers of men. One comes asking for help over some hard place in life. The one consulted sees the way through. But how does he know that there is sufficient desire, ambition, will power there to put the thing through, to carry it out successfully? So he suggests possible difficulties. Have you thought this thing through? Have you duly considered what this will demand of you? How will you manage this or that? All the while the counselor knows that these things can be done and how they can be done. While pointing out difficulties, he is hoping that the other will rise up to meet them: "I can do this," "I will attend to that." But if the will is lacking, the courage to face tests is not adequate, then he knows that it is futile for him to go farther. He must have a courageous and a co-operating will.

Just so, in this story, did Jesus deal with the Syrophoenician woman. I contrast this touching argument with the way Jesus met the keenest intellects in Jerusalem. When they argued with him, just before he had left Judea to go into Tyre and Sidon, with how sharp a weapon he rent their snares, and turned their arguments to their confusion. And here we find him inviting, leading on, preparing the way in an argument which he wanted to lose in order that he might do what this woman wanted him to do. The poor broken-hearted woman whose name has perished is the only one of whom we read on the pages of the gospel who ever won an argument with Jesus: "Such a victory as a loving father allows to his eager child when he raises gentle obstacles and even assumes a transparent mask of harshness, but never passes the limit of the trust and love which he is probing." [2]

[2] "The Expositor's Bible," *St. Mark, in loco.*

"A transparent mask of harshness." There we get the key to this extraordinary interview. The woman saw through it. She saw behind it. She could tell from the look on his face, from the love that lay within the words that he spoke. She knew; she understood. Her faith bore the test. She had ready the answers that he wanted her to give.

"I am not sent but unto the lost sheep of the house of Israel." There was the first difficulty. She lay outside of the self-imposed sphere of his influence, beyond the prescribed limits of his ministry. But how are we to understand this? Why should Jesus, according to his own words, have confined his work to the Jews? The idea that he had not himself as yet outgrown the concept of nationalism which was the accepted dogma of his people must be dismissed at once. He challenged and denied that dogma in his earliest reported sermon in the synagogue at Nazareth—denied it, too, at the peril of his life. From the beginning religion for him was a thing of the spirit that knew no frontiers, and his gospel was for all mankind. The only remaining conclusion, therefore, is that from deep and controlling motives he focused his own personal efforts upon the people of his own land, upon "the lost sheep of the house of Israel." Here we find disclosed an element in the strategy of Jesus which is often overlooked. His life had concentration, precision. He ordered his life with the most careful calculation, that it might produce the deepest and most permanent results.

From this point of view, certain phrases in the gospel narrative become invested with new, solemn, and even tragic significance. What courage and control lay behind the words: "Into any city of the Samaritans enter ye not." Why not? Were there not in that city those who were waiting for what he only could do for them? for his compassionate ministry? Why did he not go into that city and give to it what he had so freely given to others? For the reason that this lay just beyond his powers. It was more than with his human strength he could do. That strength was never overtaxed. There is no hint in the record of Jesus' life of a depleted physical or nervous energy. His strength was always sufficient for his task. And that was due in part to the courageous limitation of that task, to the deliberate elimination of everything that lay beyond its self-imposed boundaries.

Thus we understand the meaning of the words: "I am not sent but unto the lost sheep of the house of Israel." He was indeed the Saviour of all men, and knew that he was. But how best could he perform that universal mission? By concentrating his attention on the few, not by seeking to reach the many. He would firmly plant the Truth which he had come to reveal in the hearts of a handful of men whom he had chosen to be his disciples and then by them and through them that Truth would find its way to the ends of the earth. Twelve, seventy, a hundred and twenty-five—but these would be the heralds of salvation to the Gentiles, to whom he himself in his own person would not come. Thus there would be no dissipation of energy; rather it would be concentrated within certain rigid limits, applied to certain definite ends.

Look within the lives of all efficient workers for the welfare of their fellow men, and you will find the same heroic limitation of their energy. To work well, it is necessary to have a due sense of proportion, a sense of relative values. There must be one central and supreme objective. We recall how Jesus said to Pilate, "To this end was I born." Or how Paul said, "This one thing I do." All great lives are built around one central idea. There must be, in efficient living, this severe definition of the central and controlling purpose. Then must be considered the relation of the many things to the one thing. These must be sifted deliberately and courageously. One must delete secondary things which, however interesting and important in themselves, would prevent the fine performance of the main purpose. Many people fail to live their lives most advantageously at just this point. They fail because of the unrelated miscellaneousness of their lives. They attempt too much. They spread their energies over so broad an area that they do not really fructify any part of it. What is needed is the imitation in their lives of the high strategy of the life of Jesus. They must survey the whole field of their possible usefulness, mark off the sphere of their best influence, and then deliberately decline many other possible opportunities for service which lie beyond the frontiers of time and strength.

The fact needs to be faced that, given a person of ordinary health, devotion, and capacity, there will come to him more appeals for aid, more opportunities for service than he can wisely heed. In the ordering of his life, therefore, there is needed the courageous concentration that we discover in the life of Jesus. Every life must have what we may call its major course, chosen with deliberation and conscious consecration. And from many another path of service, from many another avenue of influence, one will turn resolutely aside in order in this way and by this means the better to glorify God and to serve

141

one's fellow men. Character, it has been well said, is more fundamental than reputation. There is therefore an absolute necessity of boldly throwing overboard many things, if superficiality and thinness of character and of performance are to be avoided. As Emerson said, "The one prudence in life is concentration, the one evil is dissipation." Carlyle was right when he wrote that the weakest living creature by concentrating his powers on an object can accomplish something; the strongest, by dispersing his over many, may fail to accomplish anything.

"I am not sent but unto the lost sheep of the house of Israel." How was the poor woman to overcome this difficulty? She did it by the elevation of herself. "Lord, help *me*." How beautiful, how unutterably eloquent that was. Here, she said, am I. She raised herself above all the rest of humanity in presenting her stark, solitary, demanding necessity to the soul of Jesus. And that was irresistible. That always must be irresistible. No matter what our particular task may be, the crying necessity of *any one,* no matter how far he may seem to lie outside the sphere of our interest, must command our immediate attention. The claim of any human soul in desperate need is instant and supreme. Yet Jesus

142

put one more test before this suppliant woman. He reminded her that, according to the rigid exclusiveness of his own people, for a Jew to give his spiritual possessions to a Gentile would be like taking food that belonged to children and throwing it to the dogs. It sounds harsh and unfeeling. Without doubt, however, the words were uttered in a way and with a look which showed plainly that Jesus himself did not subscribe to the dogma, well understood by the woman, which limited the sympathy of his countrymen. Moreover, when Jesus used the word "dog" he was not referring to the savage, scavenger dogs that prowled about the streets. The word used in this passage is a diminutive. The same word is used by both Matthew and Mark. It is found nowhere else in the New Testament. It means little dogs, pet dogs. Thus a simple domestic scene is called to mind. I can imagine a smile on Jesus' face as he suggests the picture: the children at table who are not allowed to feed the pet doggies who clamor for food. All harshness is taken from the passage at once when thus understood. It was a gentle and not a stern word that was uttered. And the woman was quick to perceive this. She entered at once into the meaning of the picturesque scene that Jesus had sketched, and with quick wit she replied: "True

143

enough, but even the doggies do have something to eat when the children have done with their meal." It is one of the sweetest dialogues in the Gospels. Rightly understood, it is a thing of sentiment and of beauty.

Then Jesus answered: "Great is thy faith: be it unto thee even as thou wilt." He had tested her, and he had found that which he needed, which he hoped and longed to find—a heart humble, believing, strong, and pure.

It is for lack of this prevailing faith, of this abounding hope, that more cures are not wrought either for those whom we love, or for ourselves. We become easily discouraged, we are unable to surmount the difficulties that lie in our path. We despair of the possibility of bringing about the desired results. We doubt, we falter. And at last we cease to hope at all. It is for us all, then, that the piteous story of this unknown Syrophoenician woman is set down on the pages of the Gospels. To think of it! She can teach us all, teach us that no case is too desperate for prayer. For there, behind our need, He stands mighty to save. So let us persevere, meet every challenge, every difficulty, with the stubborn unwavering faith that he can do what he did for this poor unknown woman so long ago.

144

CHAPTER EIGHT

THE RICH YOUNG MAN

MATTHEW 19:16-22; MARK 10:17-22; LUKE 18:18-23

IT WAS NEAR THE END OF THE PUBLIC MINISTRY of Jesus. He was on his way to Jerusalem for the last time. As he was starting a new day's journey, a young man detached himself from the crowd and, as the Gospel of Mark tells us, with its vivid and picturesque touches, ran to him and kneeled before him as was usual before a venerated rabbi. The other two Gospels tell us all that we know about this young man: that he was rich, and a ruler of the synagogue. These rulers of the synagogue were church officers; they administered its affairs like members of a church board today. But, since church and state were one, they were civil magistrates also, members of the Sanhedrin. They were elected by the congregation. Thus this young ruler must have been much esteemed, popular, a man of reputation. Every line that is drawn in his portrait reveals a noble and attractive personality.

What caused such a man to come to Jesus like that, stepping out from the crowd, making himself

145

conspicuous, and publicly showing such reverence to Jesus? Doubtless he yielded to an impulse. He had long watched Jesus, had been attracted by him, felt in the depths of his nature that this itinerant Rabbi could answer the deepest questions and satisfy the deepest longings of his own spiritual life. There is revealed here, as in a flash, the impression which Jesus made upon the minds of the most thoughtful, the most cultured men of his time, those who were most sensitive to spiritual things. He attracted them as by a magnet. He drew them irresistibly to himself. Thus it happened that this cultured and aristocratic young ruler, a tumult of emotion in his heart, ran to him and knelt before him. It was not only a sensational thing to do. It was also perilous. The authorities were now in such open opposition to Jesus that the man must have known that he was taking his social and political future in his hands when he did such a thing, openly avowing his belief in the goodness of the Master. Yet no fear held him back. He felt in his heart that there was some great secret which Jesus could reveal. For "the peace of God sat visibly on his brow."

It is an appealing picture. There is hardly another in all the Gospels to match it. He, too, was in need. But he was not a cripple, a notorious sinner, or blind or diseased. On the contrary, he was in the prime and strength of his fine young manhood. Neither did he come on behalf of another. He came for himself. And it was not intellectual difficulty that brought him to Jesus as in the case of Nicodemus. His need was inward and spiritual. After everything that home and breeding and education and success in life had done for him, he felt an inward dissatisfaction; knew that there was a spiritual reality beyond all that which he had reached; an experience of God that was not his; a fullness and richness of life of which in Jesus he had a vision, which he did not know how to attain. In spite of all that was his, all that he possessed, despite too the opinion that other people had of him, his position, respectability, and all the rest, he knew that there was a Kingdom of Heaven into which he had not entered. There was an unsatisfied longing, a yearning for a better, higher life which he knew was above him and beyond him. Thus there is presented to us a case of need different from any which we have thus far met in these stories of how Jesus dealt with men.

We may well study it carefully, for there are many young men and women in our modern world who are in the precise position in which this young man

147

found himself. They have good family background and traditions. They have lived clean moral lives. They listen to the arguments of their sophisticated friends who justify their conduct by plausible theory, yet themselves adhere to their own austere standards by choice and conviction. They are upright, honest, educated in the intellectual disciplines, well-read, cultured. Also religion has a place in their lives. They were brought up that way, and although they may have revised or abandoned altogether certain ways of formulating religious truth or even certain religious habits, still they have never divested themselves of religious ideas and attitudes. Moreover, they are thinking about the biggest things in life. They are facing its problems, grappling with its gravest issues. They are seeking the highest good. They are morally in earnest, living by the best they know.

And yet they are not satisfied. They may conceal this sense of frustration beneath an apparent contentment, yet it is there. There is a beyond to which they have not attained. They do not know just what it is, or where it is, or how they can possess it. But beyond the findings of science there is the eternal mystery; beyond all sensible things, the infinite beauty; beyond all their moralities, the horizons of

148

holiness; beyond success or outward attainment, an elusive reality; beyond the actual, the ideal. They are aware of a chasm which yawns between what they are or what they have done and Truth itself, to know which is their deepest passion. "A spiritual glory, undefined and indefinable, floats before the eyes of men whom the God of this world has not blinded." [1] They seek to understand it and to know it for themselves. They read the books of the best guides and teachers that they can find. They haunt the churches, listening for some word, some note that will reveal this reality to them, or they go to some one of their friends who seems to possess what they know they lack, and ask the passionate question: "What must I do to have for myself the life that I see and know in you?" In some such fashion as this the young man in our story is the prototype of many a youth today who, seemingly possessing everything, knows that he still lacks the one thing needful. And he brought his need to Jesus himself. Seeing and feeling that in Jesus lay the secret which he had longed to know, he ran and knelt at his feet and cried: "Good Master, what shall I do that I may inherit eternal life?"

It was the identical question which the lawyer

[1] "The Expositor's Bible," *St. Mark, in loco.*

149

asked who "tempted" Jesus, and drew from him the immortal parable of the good Samaritan.[2] Yet how poles apart the two questions actually were. Here we have an illustration of how identical words can have opposite meanings. To the shrewd lawyer they presented an academic question in seeking to answer which Jesus might find himself involved in difficulty. Behind the words lay only the motive of cunning and concealed malice. But when the young man asked the question in the same words, it came from a heart passionately seeking an answer to the innermost problem of his own experience. How now will Jesus deal with him? We follow every word in this extraordinary and critical dialogue, feeling that we are here in the midst of decisive issues, that we are listening to words that are indeed heart-searching, upon which the moral future not only of this young ruler but our very own may be said to depend.

Jesus' first words seem surprising. They have given rise to much misunderstanding and even of theological controversy. Yet, in reality, Jesus could begin in no other way. The young man had called him "Good Master." The implication was that Jesus was primarily a rabbi, a teacher, outstanding in virtue and in wisdom. Yet here was a fundamen-

[2] Luke 10:25-37.

tally wrong idea. Merely as a teacher, as an instructor in morals and religion, Jesus could not help this young man. He had not come to prescribe a new ethics; he had come to transmit a new kind of life. So long as the young man felt that it was as a Master, pre-eminently good, that Jesus could solve his problem, that problem would never be solved. He must learn first of all to look upon Jesus not as a Good Master, but as the possessor of that eternal life which the young man yearned to have, which Jesus alone could give him. So Jesus tells him that goodness is of God alone, and that the goodness which the youth saw and felt to be in Jesus came from God. It was Jesus' own way of saying what is the uniform confession of the New Testament concerning him; that "in him was life, and the life was the light of men."

Here, then, is the first prerequisite for any receiving of the divine gift of eternal life upon the part of any earnest seeker after it. It is not something to be learned; it is something to receive. It is not taught; it is caught. The fugitive life and glory for which we seek is to be ours, not by any precept or form of instruction, but by the putting of our lives into communication with the Source of all life, and thus we receive it by the invisible process of transmission and acceptance. "Walking by his grace in the way of holiness is the path to life."

Again, the young man's question involved another error. He imagined that in order to gain the life he longed to know, there was something more for him to do, some added word of law and commandment of which he was unaware for him to keep or to fulfill. And Jesus proceeded to address himself to this mistaken idea. Often in his dealing with men, Jesus began with what he felt to be in their hearts, thus leading them to the higher truth which it was his purpose to convey. He did so in this case. He knew that there was nothing more for this young man to do in the sense in which the question was asked, but he began just at that point. "What must you do? But you know the commandments." Jesus' answer did not satisfy the young man and Jesus knew that it would not satisfy him. He was expecting to hear some new and special requirement, demanding pain and effort, the keeping of which might put in his hand the key to the Kingdom. When Jesus therefore told him to keep the commandments, he answered, "Which?" What command did Jesus especially mean? And to his astonishment and mortification, instead of naming some new and higher injunction, Jesus simply repeated the well-known words of that part of the Decalogue which enjoined man's duty to man, concluding, according to Matthew, with the words: "Thou shalt love thy neighbor as thyself."

Again, this was the identical answer which Jesus gave to the lawyer when he asked his question. But how differently was Jesus' answer received. The lawyer, we read, seeking a way out for himself, asked the question, "Well, who would you say is my neighbor?" But the young man's reply came from his very heart: "But, Master, this is just the point. I have kept all of these commandments from my youth up, and still I do not feel that I possess eternal life." Here is no hint of pride or of self-righteousness. Here is the open statement of fundamental truth. A man may have kept all the requirements of the moral law and still feel himself to be outside the Kingdom of Heaven.

The juxtaposition of certain passages in the Gospels is often very striking. In the Gospel of Luke, just before this story, occurs the parable of the Pharisee and the publican. Here are two men, almost side by side, who make an identical assertion. The Pharisee thanked God that he was not like others who had not kept the commandments, whereas he had done so. And in him we see the pride and self-complacency of the self-righteous man. A few verses below and we find the rich young ruler asserting the same thing of himself. Yet how opposite is the attitude of the two men. The one feels that because he has kept law and commandment, he is accepted of God, while the other knows that although he has kept them, he has not inherited eternal life. No wonder that Jesus loved the young man, charming in his frankness, humble and teachable, eager for a higher life, asking in all earnestness, "What shall I do, what lack I yet?"

"Then Jesus beholding him loved him, and said unto him, One thing thou lackest." Love preceded criticism. That is why the criticism was not resented. The young man may have gone away sorrowful, but he did not go away angry. For he knew that behind the judgment there lay the love that prompted it. In our dealings with men it is well to remember that only as we love them, and as they know that we love them, will they receive our words of criticism and judgment without resentment. Let love be lacking, and though our judgment be just, and though men know it to be just, it will arouse feelings of animosity and of indignation. But let love be there, we may say what we will. We may tell them that they are foolish, improvident, self-

154

indulgent, blameworthy, and they will receive our judgment of them humbly and even thankfully, knowing this to be true, knowing too that it is out of our love for them that we speak as we do. Only one who truly loves another can safely tell him what he lacks.

For a love that is real is at the same time stern. The penetrating eye of Jesus pierced to the source of the malady in the soul of this youth. Like a skillful surgeon, he proposed to cut beneath every tissue until he had removed the disease at its very roots. Had he not loved him so much, he might have stopped short of that. It was precisely his love that caused him to utter the words that revealed to the young man, perhaps for the first time, what it was that stood between him and that Kingdom into which he longed to enter. In our dealings with men a genuine love for them will always have within it this same element of an uncompromising thoroughness. Only a love that is superficial, flaccid, sentimental ever stops short of a stern demand for the surrender of whatever is needed for the recovery of that completeness of spiritual health which alone spells salvation.

"Go thy way, sell whatsoever thou hast, and give to the poor, and thou shalt have treasure in heaven."

The words fell on the mind and heart of the young man with the blow of an abrupt and sudden surprise. He himself had not been aware of the stealthy fashion in which his love of wealth had grown upon him until it had eclipsed his complete love of God. Ruskin has sketched the growth of this malady of money-making:

That is an all-absorbing game, and it is absolutely without purpose. No one who ever heartily engages in that game, ever knows why. Ask a great money-maker what he wants to do with his money, he never knows. He doesn't make it to do anything with it. He gets it only that he may get it. "What will you make of what you have got?" you ask. "Well, I'll get more," he says. Just as at cricket you get more runs. There is no use in the runs, but to get more of it than other people is the game.

It was so with this youth. The love of money-getting had become a major passion that unconsciously to himself had absorbed the higher energies of his being. His possessions stood between him and the possession of eternal life. There lay the answer of Jesus to the young man's earnest question, "What must I do, beyond what already I have done, to know the kind of life I see in you, into which I myself long to enter?" And this will be the answer today to anyone who asks: "How can I capture the radiance and the beauty, the glory and the peace that lie beyond all secular knowledge and conventional morality?" That must be removed which prevents the full entrance into the soul of the Life of God. That Life lies all about us, seeking to flood our being in all its parts—mind, soul and body— with its regenerating power. The Light in its brightness seeks to shine through the windows of the soul and reveal all manner of hidden virtue and beauty. Only when obstacles have been removed that prevent the entrance of that Life; only when darkened windows have been cleaned of all that hinders the through-shining of that Light, can the soul know that fullness of life for which it longs.

If, then, one feels dissatisfied as did this young man; if one longs for a fuller life than, with all his other endowments, he feels he knows; if one yearns to know the secret of a life so abundant that it bequeaths a peace that passes understanding, let him, so teaches Jesus in his dealing with this youth, search his heart for that other love, whatever it may be, that thwarts the full entrance into his life of the perfect love of God. To find our way to God, it is necessary only to allow God to find his way to us. When once whatever stands in the way of this seeking Love of us is removed, we do not so much enter into eternal life; it enters into us.

From this point of view, privilege of any kind constitutes a moral danger, for it projects a possible barrier between us and the seeking Life of God. It is an obstacle to that humble, receptive, and trusting spirit which is ready to receive what God seeks to share. It breeds self-sufficiency, a pride of possession, and tends to develop a love for what one has attained and is not willing to surrender. Therefore it is easier for the underprivileged than for the privileged to inherit eternal life. Jesus made his own commentary on this truth when he said: "How hardly shall they that have riches enter into the kingdom of God!"

This young ruler was rich in money. But there are other ways of being rich, and the danger is always the same. One may be rich in health. It is a great possession. Yet how true it is that physical robustness often of itself makes one impenetrable to the finer things of the Spirit which are revealed to those who lack it. Also he is tempted to inconsiderateness, and by the very exuberance of his own vitality he depletes or exhausts the strength of others weaker than he. Fine family life, ancestry, and traditions are great riches. Yet they are forms of wealth in which there lie grave moral perils. They tend to breed a sense of exclusiveness and of superiority to others, to develop a kind of caste conceit, even to create a feeling that birth of itself admits one into the Kingdom of Heaven. Family pride is a fine thing, yet it often tends to remove one to a distance from the homeless and the friendless and to dry up the springs of human brotherhood and sympathy. It is possible also to attain such a degree of respectability that the suggestion of penitence would be considered to be an impertinence. Education is a great possession, the acquirement of culture and refinement, of the disciplined intellect and the trained mind. Here indeed are great riches. Yet here also lies moral peril. For these often breed a state of mind which has little to do with the Beatitudes. The habit of the scholar, even of the educated man, is to look at all forms of experience as things to be critically examined, without even contemplating the possibility of losing oneself in any one of them. The purely academic type of mind seems often to be impervious to the entrance of spiritual truth.

The devout spirit is not fed by purely intellectual processes; sometimes it is even frustrated by them. It was a saying of Dr. Arnold, certainly no disparager of the intellect, that no student could long continue in a healthy religious state unless his heart was kept tender by mingling with children or by frequent intercourse with the poor and the suffering. . . . . If he is ever to get beyond the outer precinct and pass within the holy place, he must put off his critical apparatus and enter as a simple, contrite-hearted man. Not as men of science but as little children shall we enter the kingdom of heaven.[3]

Always there is the menacing possibility that the training of the intellect, the sharpening of the critical faculty, shall somehow come to dominate and to control the other and no less authentic elements of personality—the emotions, the responsive and tender heart, the sense of dependence and need, which, all taken together and fused into a living whole, make one to be a citizen of the Kingdom of Heaven. Once more, the possession of power, of initiative, of influence, of ability to sway the minds and command the loyalties of other men—this also is great wealth. There are few joys in life comparable to the consciousness that we can bring things to pass. But such riches have their grave moral dangers: the danger of pride, imperiousness, self-aggrandisement, disregard of others, obstinacy, temptation always to

[3] J. C. Shairp, *Culture and Religion*, Houghton Mifflin Co., 1893, pp. 125, 127. Used by permission.

the use of power for selfish ends. A sense of power is, in reality, one of the most perilous forms of wealth. Like the passion for money-getting it is a kind of poison which infects the whole moral system. It grows by what it feeds on. For few minds are so well-balanced as to bear the strain of the possession of unlimited power without moral deterioration. All history, all biography go to prove how hardly shall they who possess such riches enter into the Kingdom of God.

Thus the trenchant judgment of Jesus in the case of the rich young ruler finds its complete vindication. Every possession in life has these two aspects. It is on the one hand a privilege, on the other hand a peril, an obstacle that may bar one from the Kingdom of Heaven. If we have perhaps unconsciously thus misused it, there is but one thing for us to do. We must sell all that we have in one determined purpose to give all that we are and have to God. Not only must we renounce every secret fault, passion, and ambition which conflicts with our perfect love of him. Also we must strip off both pride and prejudice. Precisely as St. Francis in one symbolic act sold all that he had, so must we divest ourselves of those inmost traits and habits of mind and heart which great possessions have made to be the gar-

161

ment of our souls, which prevent the seeking love of God from finding us and filling us with its riches, the riches of his Eternal Life.

Already I have referred to the suggestive sequence of certain passages in the Gospels. The final answer to the eager question of the rich young man is really to be found in the touching scene which just preceded his dramatic approach to Jesus. They had brought young children unto him and he had blessed them and then had said: "Whosoever shall not receive the kingdom of God as a little child, he shall not enter therein." The childlike heart: there is the condition of the inheritance of eternal life.

[This child's heart] is a very simple thing, so simple that worldly men are apt either not to perceive it or to despise it. If we allow the world to rob us of it, as so many do, we may be sure that the world has nothing equal to it to give us instead. And the only way to preserve it, is to open the heart to simple, trustful communion with God and Christ and to try to bring the heart ever closer and closer to Him. In all the best men you meet, perhaps the thing that is most peculiar about them is the child's heart which they bear within the man's. However they may differ in other respects . . . . in this they are agreed.[4]

[4] *Ibid,* pp. 130-131.

And as little children they have entered the Kingdom of Heaven.

Thus dealt Jesus with this young man whom he loved. And so must all wise helpers of men deal with those who, having many possessions, still yearn for the unsearchable riches which lie beyond their grasp. We read that the young man went away sorrowful. Yet this may not be the end of the story. That godly sorrow may have done its perfect work for him. Haunted by the Jesus he had seen, by the words that he had spoken, unable to resist the persuasion that here for him lay indeed the way to life eternal, may he not in later days have obeyed, and so have found the peace for which he longed?

CHAPTER NINE

THE BLIND MAN

JOHN 9:1-38

THERE IS NOT MUCH OF THEOLOGY OR OF ABstract statement of truth to be found in these four little books which tell us all that we know of the earthly life of Jesus. Rather the truth is presented to us in story and in anecdote, in the parables and in these concrete and picturesque accounts of how Jesus dealt with men and women in the varied vicissitudes of life. These stories are very simple. They are also very profound. They may be read in a few minutes, but they plumb to the depths. If one reads them carefully and reverently one discovers in them the deepest spiritual truths. They are really parables; and this story of the giving of sight to the man who was born blind is a parable of the spiritual life. It is one of the most interesting, the most vivacious, stories to be found in the Gospels. One admires the man who is its central figure. There was something racy in his character; he was not without a touch of good-humored satire, ready-witted and by no means devoid of logic. And he was a man of courage.

"And as Jesus passed by, he saw a man." To understand the situation and to grasp its full significance, we should read the last verse in the previous chapter. He was in Jerusalem, in the midst of his enemies now bent on his destruction. Enraged at his teaching, they had taken up stones to throw at him. But Jesus, we read, went through the midst of them and so passed by.

It was at such a moment that he saw this man. Confronted by the sinister and deadly hate of his foes, he still had eyes for one of the most commonplace sights in Palestine. The blinding sun, the white and dusty highways, the absence of proper medical care, have combined to this day to make blindness startlingly prevalent in the Holy Land. But Jesus in the days of his Passion was not so preoccupied that He failed to see the pathetic figure of this otherwise robust young man who had been blind from his birth.

We find here a dramatic and reiterated illustration of the method of Jesus in his mission of redemption. We learn here one of the deepest lessons for the ordering of our lives in relation to our fellow men. "As he passed by." That seems from beginning to end to have been Jesus' way of doing good. He was forever doing acts of kindness and of love to individual men and women "as he passed by." It was as he passed by that he saw Levi sitting at the place of toll. It was as he passed by that he heard the lepers calling. It was as he passed by that he felt a woman touch him, saw the impotent man at the Pool of Bethesda and Zacchaeus in his tree. Jesus did not have to go out of his way to do good, simply because the everyday road was filled with opportunities for the doing of his redemptive work.

Why do we not imitate the method of Jesus? We have the same opportunities that he had to do good to people as we pass by. The way along which Jesus walked was the same ordinary road which we follow every day of our lives. And there are plenty of people with whom we come in contact as we pass along who need what we can give if only we could see what Jesus saw "as he passed by." Sometimes people bemoan the fact that they have no time to be of service to their fellow men. The days are filled with routine work; their life is a round of monotonous and unimaginative toil. There is nothing romantic about their existence. Yet how romantic was the life of Jesus as he passed along the dusty roads and highways of Judea and Galilee! What he saw and

166

what he did, the response that he evoked, the lives made free and glad—all this made up the joy, the poetry, the romance of his life. And just this can put romance in the humblest life today. It does not take much to give happiness to people; to bring a smile on a worn, wan face; to speak a word of courage and of hope. "Little acts of thoughtfulness, broken words that have cheer and friendliness at the heart of them, deeds that make for happiness, little surprises and unexpected favors, these are within the reach of us all, and they are angels of mercy in disguise." A well-known character in one of William J. Locke's novels calls himself a "maréchand de bonheur," a dealer, a dispenser of happiness. This, perhaps, is the highest of all forms of service, and it is open to us all.

Jesus, then, was not so preoccupied by the really perilous position in which at the moment he found himself, that he failed to see this simple case of human need. But what did he see? He saw a man. The chances are that the disciples did not see him at all. If they did, all that they saw was a blind man. And there is a difference between seeing a blind man or seeing a man blind. Blindness in those days was not only a hopeless but a degrading disease, as the context shows. Thus, for the Oriental a blind man ceased to be a man. But not for Jesus. His eyes pierced beneath the outward destitution and saw the latent manhood there. And how much of a man he saw the whole story goes on to show. Always that was the method of Jesus in dealing with men. It has even been affirmed that Jesus was the first person on this planet who ever truly saw a man. He saw one here, and brought to light a soul so utterly simple and stark in its sincerity and courage as to rebuke learned scribe and Pharisee and to be an inspiration to you and me today.

But see what else all this involved. In the first place it meant quick, undulled sensitiveness to suffering, so that this commonplace spectacle of need made its instant appeal. And there is something divine in that. Again, it meant isolating this individual at once from the mass. Always there is danger that the separate personality shall be lost in the crowd. We see the throngs, but do we see the separate, sentient suffering personalities who have the same dread of pain, the same longing for happiness that we have, of whom the throngs are composed. It takes always a special form of spiritual sight and intuition to see not the impersonal multitude, but the separate person. The genius of Jesus did just

168

that, and this was the secret of his incomparable ministry to men. He let the full power of his personality fall on the individual who had been distinguished from the mass. Here then are great qualities of insight, imagination, and faith in men. Upon their possession all truly helpful ministries depend.

We see already how far this story goes. But it goes much farther. When Jesus saw that man he stopped and looked at him. So the disciples stopped and looked too. And what did they say? "Master, for whose sin was this man born blind? For his own, or for that of his parents?" That was all. Here was no word of compassion. Rather, his destitution was for them proof that either he had sinned or his parents. For that was the old Hebrew idea in which they had been brought up. It was still the orthodox view in the time of Jesus. Be good and you will be happy. If you are not happy, then you have not been good. The plight of this man was such that there must have been much wrongdoing somewhere. The idea does not even seem to have occurred to the disciples that if he had been born blind he could not himself have been the sinner.

Jesus instantly rejected this unjust dogma of the meaning of suffering. "It was neither for his sin

169

nor for that of his parents." No man can sin without suffering for it. But you cannot turn that proposition around and say, "No man can suffer unless he has sinned." Parents cannot sin without causing suffering for their children. But it does not follow that because children suffer, therefore their parents must have sinned. Jesus did not argue the matter. But he did throw a shining ray of light on the meaning of suffering. "Neither hath this man sinned, nor his parents; but that the works of God should be made manifest in him." The man was born blind to show what God can do in a case like this. The blind man must have heard the words—and think what they meant to him! All through the years he had been tormented by the question Why? And now he learned from the lips of Jesus that an innermost reason for his lifelong affliction was that he might be an illustration of what God can do. And whenever we wrestle with the problem of innocent suffering let us remember that the works of God can be revealed in suffering as in no other way.

They are revealed in the sufferer himself. Nothing is more divine, more unanswerably godlike, than the spectacle of a brave, enduring, undaunted soul enshrined in an infirm and suffering body. Pain, heroically borne, can persuade men of the reality of the soul as can nothing else. In a beautiful address delivered by Felix Adler years ago he gave this illustration:

When I was a boy I knew a good physician. He merited that name if ever a man did. Night and day he spent himself in the service of the poor. He never stopped to consider himself. He took very little notice of himself. One day, when he was only about thirty-five years of age, he became paralyzed. He could just raise his head a little, but for the rest he lay like a log. My good mother—whose memory be blessed—took a great interest in this physician, and, at her instigation, as a mere boy I was brought into this sick-chamber and spent many hours with the good physician; and as long as I live, the impression of that sick-chamber will not fade from my mind. Never a sign of impatience, never a word of complaint. When his only sister, to whom he was greatly attached, entered the room, there was always a smile on his wan face that presently broke in a spasm of pain when she closed the door behind her. He was a sufferer like Job—very simple in his fortitude, never pretending, never even aware that there was anything specially meritorious in his conduct.

And Dr. Adler goes on:

When men bring up to me the materialistic argument and say that we are nothing but compounds of matter —mere aggregate of whirling atoms—I think of the good doctor, and their argument so far as I am concerned falls flat. There was something else than body—something higher, grander, better—that was present in that room. I know it.

I think of Felix Adler's great mission as he combated the forces of materialism and insisted on the meaning of spiritual values in life. I remember that the unshakable conviction that these are the final reality came to him in his experience in that sickroom. And then I understand what Jesus meant when he said that the sufferer may show what God can do, that the works of God may be made plain, visible before men's eyes.

And the works of God are revealed not only in the sufferer, but in the sentiment of compassion which suffering evokes from the human soul. Wherever suffering has come from, there can be no doubt that it calls forth all that is best in human nature: sympathy, self-denial, gentleness, patience, forbearance. How many illustrations abound of these divine qualities in those who minister daily to the world's sufferers! All of these are wonderful works of God that rise far above the level of our ordinary human nature, works that would remain hidden, unrevealed, if they were not made manifest by suffering. If the man born blind had done no more than to bring from the lips of Jesus this flash of revelation on the meaning of suffering, we could understand, as could he, why he had suffered.

But this was not all that he did. After that came his healing. And he had his part to perform in working his cure. This is one of the instances in which Jesus gave the patient something to do, precisely as he told the lepers to go and show themselves to the priests.[1] This may well have been to test his faith. Willingness to co-operate is always a sign of desire and of faith. If this man had halted or faltered Jesus could have done nothing more for him. Wise helpers of men often imitate this method of Jesus. To the one looking for mental or moral or physical healing, they set uninviting, unpromising, and even distasteful tasks. He cannot see how all of this is going to help him. He may demur, decline. He is not equal to this test of his moral earnestness, of his real determination to get well, of his faith in the one to whom he has brought his trouble. But if he is, this is the beginning of his recovery.

So this man's faith was tested. Clay was put on his eyes. And he might have asked what good that would do. He was told to go and wash in the well-known pool of Siloam and his eyes would be opened.

[1] Luke 17:14.

173

And he did not ask how that could be. Instead, he started right off, and with the instinct of the blind, found his own way. He did as he was told. And he went away seeing. Naturally, he hastened to his own home. His parents must be the first to know the wonderful news, share in the rapture of his new-found sight.

Then the rumor of the thing got around. It was so incredible that some felt that the seeing man could not be the blind man they had known. The people crowded around him and asked him how his sight had been restored, and he told them—told them too that he did not know where Jesus was who had done this for him. So his neighbors took him to the Pharisees, probably fearing that if they did not they, too, might incur the hostility of the ruling class, which was now bent on destroying the influence of Jesus. The Pharisees interrogated the man, who gave the same simple straightforward account of his healing. And a great discussion was started. Jesus had done this thing, had used clay, done manual work, on the Sabbath day. Therefore he was a sinner. But how could a sinner do such a work of God as healing a man born blind? Thus they were caught in a cruel dilemma. There was only one way out of it; it must be proved that Jesus had done no such

174

thing. The man's parents, when asked, shrugged their shoulders and said that they knew nothing about it. Their son was old enough to speak for himself. But he stuck to his story. The Pharisees told him the thing was impossible, since Jesus was a sinner.

And then something august happened. We see this man, who only an hour before had been a begging blind man, facing the authorities and positively laying down the law to them. Already when the Pharisees had called Jesus a sinner, the man had had the courage to say, "I call him a prophet." And now that the accusation was repeated, the man let himself go. "You say this man is a sinner. Well, I know nothing about that. All that I know is that, whereas I was blind, now I see. You keep asking me what he did to me. I have already told you that and you would not listen to me. Do you want me to tell you over again? Are you really thinking of becoming his disciples?" Then they stormed at him. *"We* become his disciples? Indeed no. We follow Moses. It is you who have become his disciple. As for us, we do not know where this fellow comes from." "Is that so?" the man answered with sarcasm. "Now that *is* astonishing. For has he not opened my eyes? Who could have done such a thing unless God had been with him? God, we know, does not listen to sinners. He listens only to those who are devout, who obey his will. If this man were not from God, he could not have done anything."

It was sheer eloquence. It was the fearless utterance of a sincere and manly soul. How the onlookers at the scene must have gasped at the temerity of this man in thus answering and even taunting the rulers, the highest officials among them. They held their breath, for they knew, and the man knew, what would follow. "And so you would teach us, would you—you, a man born in degradation and sin?" And they excommunicated him. It was a public, formal act that deprived him of all civic and religious privilege. It made him an outcast with no further standing in the community. Only an Oriental can know what that meant.

But the man went away satisfied. He had his sight. But he had more than that. He had the satisfaction that every true man has who speaks what he knows to be the truth in the face of what he knows to be false. "That the works of God should be made manifest in him." So spoke Jesus. And in this exhibition of his splendid manhood, the works of God had indeed been revealed. Yet even this was not all. There had been revealed in his experience what is the rock-bottom assurance of faith in Christ.

"One thing I know." I am interested in the use which the Bible makes of the words, "One thing." "One thing I have desired," said the Psalmist. "One thing I do," cried the Apostle. But more eloquent than either is the word of this man who had been born blind: "One thing I know." It was an admission of ignorance regarding many things. He asserted nothing about Jesus which he had not proved for himself. He knew nothing of Jesus save that he had opened his eyes. He brushed aside all the other questions in which the Pharisees had tried to enmesh him. "Whether this or that be so, I do not know. One thing I know." And on that he could stand firm and secure. And if the man taught the Pharisees a lesson, he can teach us one also. The trouble with many a modern man and woman today is that he tries to know too much. He is disturbed by the questions which he cannot answer, by the matters concerning Jesus which he feels he cannot know. But here was a man who became a disciple who knew only one thing. And if we should really sit down and think, would it not be possible for us to find some point of contact with Jesus, some experience of him of which we could speak with conviction, of which we could say, "I know"? We remember some day in which we were tempted beyond measure. And then the face of Jesus just stood before us and we received the strength to stand firm. We remember a day when the light of our life was taken out of it, and we had tasted the bitter reality of sorrow. And then we saw Jesus come walking over the troubled sea of our life and heard him say, "Peace, it is I." And there was a great calm. We know that. Or we were self-satisfied, thanking God we were not like other men, feeling that we were quite all right, with nothing in ourselves of which we were really and heartily ashamed. And then somehow or other Jesus did upset our self-complacency and made us see what a shallow, superficial life had been ours, and there came a sudden shaft of light revealing a glory in life that we had missed, a love of which we had never dreamed, a devotion to others which we had never conceived—and this really made life over for us. And that was a real experience of Jesus. We can truly say, "One thing I know." I was blind—blind to duty, blind to self, blind to life and all that it is, all that it holds. I was blind. And now I see. He has made me see what I never saw before. Much I may not know. This I do know. And what we do know is the starting point of faith.

Our friends come and question us. And they know much more than we do about many things—about philosophy and criticism and science. And they put to us questions which we cannot answer, and pose problems which we cannot solve, which, they tell us, are all bound up with our faith in Jesus. But we have one answer left, and it is the answer of the blind man: "I do not know what you mean. I cannot answer the questions which you ask. Where this Jesus came from I do not know. Where he is, I cannot tell. How he was born, how he died, where he went, I know not. But one thing I know. One day I was blind. I could not see God. I could not see any real meaning in my life. I could not see my way. I was stumbling in darkness. But now I can see. I do not see everything. But I see much. I see enough to make life a blessed reality, and a future filled with hope. And it is he who has done this for me. One thing I know. And because I know it, I shall never fail in my allegiance to him.

> If Jesus Christ is a man—
>   And only a man—I say
> That of all mankind I cleave to him,
>   And to him will I cleave alway.

If Jesus Christ is a god—
And the only God—I swear
I will follow him through heaven and hell,
The earth, the sea, and the air! [2]

Ah! If Jesus had not paused when he saw the blind man that day. What works of God had not then been made manifest to me—the meaning of suffering, the revelation of manhood, the essense of faith.

We come to the end of the story. The sensational news of the man's excommunication had spread through the city and had reached Jesus. He understood the reason for it, understood that because of the man's unswerving loyalty to himself this had happened to him. So Jesus sought for the man. He was forever seeking men. He did not wait for men to come to him. He went out for them. In nothing perhaps does Jesus so illustrate in his own Person the heart of the God of the Bible than in this perpetual seeking after men. James Martineau once said that the difference between the God of the Bible and of all other faiths lies primarily here: that in them men are seeking after God if haply they may find him. In the Bible, from

[2] Richard Watson Gilder, "The Song of a Heathen." Used by permission of Houghton Mifflin Co.

the day of the Garden of Eden to the end of the Book of Revelation, God is seeking man. "And when [Jesus] had found him." It was with pains and even peril to himself that he found him. But find him he must. He could not leave the man like that. How Jesus must have loved him. What pride he must have felt in him. He could not let him go like that, an excommunicate because Jesus had opened his eyes. He must be sure also that he had received more than his physical sight. For the ministry of Jesus was both to men's bodies and to their souls. With him the distinction often drawn today between the social and the personal gospel did not exist. It was all one. He did not heal men's souls and leave them physically destitute. Yet neither did he ameliorate their outward condition and leave them in spiritual darkness.

And when he had found him, he asked him, Do you believe in the Son of man? [3] What was the experience of this man to be? Was it to be but the momentary, the isolated event of his miraculous cure, or was it to be a continuous, deep, and lasting faith in him who had wrought it—a faith that would accompany him all through the future vicissitudes

[3] See alternate reading in margin of Revised Version.

of his life? Was the opening of his eyes to be the beginning and not the end of his relationship to Jesus? And the heart of the man responded. He gave the only answer possible. "Who is he? Tell me, that I may believe in him." And then, in almost the identical words which he had used in talking to the woman of Samaria, Jesus made this rare revelation of himself: "You have seen him, he is talking to you." And the man replied on the instant. "Lord, I believe. And he worshipped him." The man's healing was complete.

I said at the beginning that these gospel stories, simple as they are, plumb to the depths. In this story how many of the aspects of human redemption find their full illustration! Yet we make a mistake if we read it only as the wonderful way in which Jesus was able to achieve this man's restoration to full manhood. Not one of us, if we but have the Spirit of Jesus within us and learn the method of his dealing with men, but may, as we pass by, open the eyes of many who are blind, and bring them home to God.

CHAPTER TEN

ZACCHAEUS

LUKE 19:1-10

*H*AVE WE EVER ASKED OURSELVES IF THERE may not be a suggestion of inspiration in the very sequence of the gospel narratives? Have we ever placed two of these gospel stories just as they occur, one after the other, and thought of the contrast which they present? In John's Gospel we find standing side by side the third and the fourth chapters. Both describe a personal and private conversation. Yet one could not have found in all Palestine two people who stood further apart than Nicodemus, the Jewish aristocrat, and the poor sodden woman of Samaria. Yet Jesus apparently was not aware of any change in social atmosphere. To the one he spoke the word, "Ye must be born again"; to the other, "Give me to drink."

Again, contrast the two stories found at the end of the eighteenth, and at the beginning of the nineteenth chapter of Luke's Gospel. They stand the one directly after the other. The one occurred as Jesus neared Jericho, the other when he had en-

183

tered it. In the first instance we find Jesus dealing with a blind beggar, Bartimaeus, a social outcast, a miserable zero in the slums of Jericho. And directly afterward we find him confronting Zacchaeus, who was chief among the publicans, and he was rich. So, from educated to ignorant and from poverty to wealth Jesus passed without a sign to be noted anywhere that he was conscious of these social distinctions. In the depth of his love, all men clasped hands and were brothers. It is a sure test of one's love for his fellow men. To share the love of Jesus is to know men as they are, not in the outward disguises of class or condition.

In Zacchaeus we find a new type: a prosperous man but not a happy one; fortunate in one way but most unfortunate in another. There are plenty like him. Cecil Rhodes looked with envy on General Booth of the Salvation Army. Asked once if he were happy Rhodes replied: "Happy? I happy? Good God, no! I would give all that I possess to believe what that old man believes." [1] It will repay us to study the method of Jesus in dealing with Zacchaeus. The story lies before us in these verses. It is told only by Luke. It is full of human

[1] Sarah G. Millard, *Cecil Rhodes*, p. 382.

184

interest and the narrative is not without its suggestion of humor. It has simple and homely touches that provoke a smile.

Jesus was on his way to Jerusalem for the last time. Report had spread his fame abroad, and everyone wanted to see him. How little human nature has changed. Let it be known that a person of great reputation is to pass on his way, and how quickly a crowd will gather. How eagerly many will climb poles and trees and every other place of vantage in order to see him. Zacchaeus was no exception to the rule even if he was a person of importance. He wanted to see him so much that he forgot his dignity. And because he was short, and could not see over the heads of other people, he looked around for an elevation and he found one. There was a sycamore tree near at hand, easy to climb because of its short trunk and low-growing branches. It took but a moment for Zacchaeus to lodge himself there right by the road along which Jesus was to pass.

Let us look at this man for a moment. He was a Jew, also a publican, that is, a taxgatherer. And because the Jews chafed under the taxes levied by the Roman government, and hated the government that levied them, they despised any Jew who was willing to be an agent of Rome, in collecting the taxes from the people. The government paid them well for the work, a stipend which nothing but sordid avarice would persuade a Jew to accept. Thus the very name "publican" had become a symbol of all that is base and disloyal. To this class Zacchaeus belonged. Moreover, he was chief publican. He had grown rich in the business. He made a very good thing by overcharging merchants, who rather than make costly appeals found it better to pay the blackmail and submit. Therefore, from whatever point of view we look at the man we find a particularly uninteresting type. He was the unpromising and unscrupulous man of business. There was nothing picturesque or appealing about this prosperous and renegade Jew. It might appear as if there could be no spiritual problem here.

Yet behold how universal and inclusive the appeal of the gospel is. No kind of man but is the object of the love of God which came into the world with Jesus. No type is outside the range of his interest. No heart but can be reached by his message. No man can resist his call and his claims. A gospel that can in succession touch and reach a Nicodemus, a poor blind man, and a Zacchaeus is indeed a universal gospel.

I pause for a moment to note that Jesus will use

186

what looks like a poor motive for his divine ends.
I think of how that day opened for Zacchaeus, and
how it ended. "This day is salvation come to this
house." Well, that is perhaps all that a day will
hold. A day that has brought salvation to a man
has brought him everything that a day can bring.
But there was nothing to indicate that that day was
to be different from any other. Neither did Zacchaeus act in a fashion that was likely to bring him
so rich a reward. But when Jesus comes into a
man's life in any way, that life is touched by an
influence that may fundamentally alter its attitude
and direction. And so it fell out with Zacchaeus.

"He sought to see Jesus who he was." Weymouth translates it: "He was anxious to see what
sort of man Jesus was." It would, however,
be going too far to say that sheer curiosity was all
his motive. There may have been some feeling of
reverence, some religious emotion mixed in with
this. It is hard to account for what happened without it. Men rarely act from single motives. One
who comes to church, for example, may do so partly
from custom and partly from reverence. It is in
part habit and in part desire; in part duty and in
part privilege. At bottom I dare say Zacchaeus
had some feeling of need. Still, the immediate if

not the whole motive was to get a good look at Jesus as he passed. It was not a motive as deep as that of Nicodemus, who was sincerely troubled; nor as noble as that of the rich young man who ran and fell at his feet. But Jesus took the minor motive and used it. It was enough that this man wanted to see him; wanted so much to see him that he climbed a tree to do it; that away down in his heart he knew that he was not the man he ought to be, or wanted to be. Jesus took the motive for what it was. Curiosity may have led Zacchaeus to Jesus. But it brought salvation to his house. This man who began on such a poor level, ended by being a disciple of the Lord.

"And when Jesus came to the place, he looked up, and saw him." It may have been a poor, even a ridiculous place, and yet it was the place of destiny. The history of a soul was to be made at that place. And when Jesus came to it, he looked up. What made him look up? How is it that Jesus was forever seeing people whom no one else noticed? His eyes, as Dr. Jowett once said, were eager scouts. No one but Jesus saw Levi at the place of custom. No one but Jesus saw Zacchaeus. No one cared about them. They were seen and yet not seen. They were ciphers, empty of all significance. "But Jesus

188

cared. He cared with burning eagerness and he made his quest as with searchlights which sought out every nook and corner, prying even among obscurities for treasures of his Kingdom. His passion for man determined his vision. His eyes were the servants of that passion, always and everywhere." [2] Only those who share the passion of Jesus possess his vision. Only they see men whom others do not really see at all. We recall another incident when Jesus saw a man by a tree—only not in it but under it. And Jesus then said to Nathanael: "When thou wast under the fig tree, I saw thee." Jesus saw him wrestling with some problem, in the grip of some inspiration, awake to some higher ideal of life or duty. He had not only seen him but he had seen what was in him. So here, Jesus not only saw Zacchaeus but he saw through him. Zacchaeus went out to see Jesus that day. Yet really it was Jesus who saw Zacchaeus. Jesus came to the place where this little man was perched in the tree, he looked up, read his whole story, and called to him to come down.

We are all coming to places every day where there is someone not wholly satisfied with himself, beneath

[2] J. H. Jowett.

whose apparently uninteresting exterior are motives ready to respond to the right touch, to "the rightly directed breath," so that salvation can come to his house that day. If only we could see him, see in him, see through him with the eyes of Jesus. Sight, insight, through-sight—these are great gifts. Those who possess them, when they come to the place look up and see and speak, and salvation comes to someone's house that day.

Now note what Jesus said: "Zacchaeus, make haste, and come down; for today I must abide at thy house." And the crowd that was following came to a standstill. What was this that was going on? It must have taken some courage for Zacchaeus to come down from his undignified perch in the tree with the crowd all looking on. If Jesus had simply said, "Come down," he might have hesitated. But to be told to come down because he was to be host to Jesus—this lent him all the courage he needed. He could not come down fast enough. I suppose that Zacchaeus did not have many guests in his house. It was one of the penalties he paid for his success as a crooked financier. Entertaining was out of his line. And here was Jesus. There was not a scribe or a Pharisee in Jericho who would not have been glad to have him for a guest. And he chose Zac-

190

chaeus instead. It is difficult to know whether the
crowd or Zacchaeus was the more surprised. The
crowd wondered whether Jesus knew that the host
he had chosen was a disreputable man whose business was past speaking about. And Zacchaeus was
surprised too, but his was a surprise of joy. "And he
made haste, and came down, and received him
joyfully."

Jesus, then, won the heart of Zacchaeus by asking
a favor of him. He who was about to confer a favor
began by asking one. He was about to do a great
work for Zacchaeus, but he began by asking Zacchaeus to do something for him. It was a method
which Jesus often used and it never failed. He
asked the woman at the well for a drink of water.
He ended by giving her the water of life. He asked
for the hospitality of the home at Bethany. He
brought into it the resurrection and the life. His
appeal to man was not only on their need of him,
but also on his need of them. A true relationship,
Jesus understood, is reciprocal. Real communion
cannot be all on one side. Nothing is so paralyzing
as the perpetual receiving of benefits. Nothing
makes the heart of a real man so glad as to be told
that there is something that he can *do*. Had Jesus
told Zacchaeus to come down from that tree, told

him too what a rascally sinner he was, and had asked him if he did not want to be saved, Zacchaeus might have been cornered, but he would have remained unimpressed and unmoved. But here was Jesus telling him to come down and get dinner ready for him, because he would be his guest!

Those who would help their fellow men would do well to lay this lesson to heart. We tell men how much they need God. Will we never tell them how much God needs them? We remind them how much Christ can do for them. Will we never tell them how much, if they are willing, they can do for Christ? It comes like a revelation into many a man's life that there is something that he can do which, if left undone, will leave Jesus hungry. There are hundreds of men like Zacchaeus up all kinds of trees in their religious and Christian thinking. And only one thing will bring them down—to be told that some of Christ's purposes halt and falter, some of his needs go unsatisfied without them; that he has something which only they can do for him. Let them hear a word like that and they will climb right down from their trees and joyfully receive him. We must make the appeal to all that is willing and gallant in man. Dr. McLaren has pointed out that "There is always an emphasis of love or

warning or authority in Christ's use of men's names."
Probably no one outside his own class had ever
held out his hand to Zacchaeus in all his life before,
and the kindness was as sweet as it was strange. The
emphasis here is one both of authority and of love.
The strange deep longings in the soul of this man
were read by Jesus, and he made the one irresistible
appeal. We never escape the note of joy in Jesus'
dealing with men. He put a song in the mouth of
all, the most discouraged, neglected and depressed.
The music of the gospel, the music it evokes, the
way it makes the heart to sing, proves it to be true.

We come now to the dramatic and decisive moment in this story. We must imagine Zacchaeus giving his orders, the places provided, the feast prepared, the Guest made welcome. Zacchaeus and
Jesus are by themselves at last. What took place
between them while they ate we are not told. We
are told only what happened when the feast was
over. Jesus had uttered no word of reproach or
condemnation. He had simply showed his love of
the man, and held before him the image of his own
pure and unsullied life. And the effect was instan-
taneous and decisive. Down in the soul of Zacchaeus
had lain this felt dissatisfaction with himself,
with his life, with all that he had been and done;

193

and, the feast over, obeying an uncontrollable impulse, he suddenly rose and came and stood before Jesus, who, I repeat, had spoken no word of judgment or reproach, and made his grand and complete recantation—came his complete repentance. Unlike the rich young man, he capitulated entirely. "Master, you know I have not been a very good man. I have done some very unjust deeds in my life. I realize now what a terrible business this has been. I am sick and tired of it. I never liked it, but I hadn't the heart to give it up. I am throwing it all up here and now. I have made my money by cruel exactions. I have sold my soul. Now I am going to make restitution. Before beginning my new life I must make compensation for the wrongs I have done. I shall give the poor whom I have wronged half of my possessions and every other man wronged shall have his money restored fourfold." And when the man had finished, Jesus said, "This day is salvation come to this house." The great day had come. Henceforth it would be a new life. He would be a new creature. It had been a great conversation, which ended in a great decision. Zacchaeus would never forget that day, the day he had set out to see Jesus, the day that Jesus had seen him.

Now I am glad that Jesus used that word
194

"salvation," because here we have Jesus' own definition of what salvation is. It is astonishing today what vague and confused ideas people have about the meaning of salvation. Probably if many people were to speak their minds on the subject, the idea of salvation would be bound up with some kind of rhapsody, some great emotional experience. One must pass through various forms of obscure inward feelings in order to experience salvation. But look at this story and see what salvation means.

Well, first of all it meant for Zacchaeus one great comprehensive realization of the kind of man he really was. I have often tried to picture that scene to myself. One has to fill in the details because the gospel narrative leaves them to the imagination. But I can see Zacchaeus in the presence of Him in whom the secrets of all hearts are revealed, suddenly realizing what he was. As a matter of fact, he had become the victim of one of the most deadly of sins, a sin that like a canker had eaten the heart out of him. He had made an idol of money until it had warped and ruined his nature. It had hardened and it had blighted him. All of his better feelings had given way to it, even the deep-seated love of esteem so natural to the human heart. For the sake of it he had been willing to become a virtual outcast

195

among his own people, and to be regarded as a renegade and a traitor. There are no lengths to which
men will not go when the sinister passion for wealth
has once fastened on them, and Zacchaeus had gone
all lengths. He may have begun by drifting into it;
more likely he chose it. He must have known that
he was doing a great wrong. His own better nature
and his friends must all have tried to keep him from
it. He had to stifle conviction and conscience in
order to become a publican and a chief publican.
And now, in the presence of Christ, it all swept over
him; confronted by holiness he understood his mean-
ness and his sin. He got a good look at himself in
the glass and he recoiled from it. He saw his own
heart for the first time and he did not like the look
of it.

That was the first step with Zacchaeus. And this
is the way that salvation is linked up with the Person
of Jesus. There is nothing mystical about it and
there is nothing magical about it. It simply means
that the soul of Jesus is a mirror in which one can
see what manner of man one is. Zacchaeus started
that day by wanting to see what kind of a man Jesus
was. He ended it by seeing what kind of a man
he himself was. Jesus dealt with him by offering
him the opportunity of self-revelation. And it has

been so ever since. We go along day by day acquiring, as Zacchaeus did, consciously and unconsciously, all kinds of habits, dispositions, propensities. We do not realize this subtle coloring of our natures by their gradual effect upon us. And then one day we confront Holiness either in the person of Jesus himself or in the person of one whom he has made holy; and then we see what we really are. That is why, when Jesus came into the house of Zacchaeus that day, salvation came unto it.

But in the next place, there came—came on the instant, came with irresistible force—the great resolution. It reached down to the bottom. It tore acquired habit up by the roots. It did in a moment an all but impossible thing. For perhaps the hardest thing in the world is to get a man of the world to do what Zacchaeus did then and there. The whole nature of the man was put behind his new inspiration to godliness. He rose to the height of his moral stature. He may have been a little man in one way, but there is no mistaking the grandeur of his soul. Strength, ability, thoroughness—these he must have possessed. He had put them to a bad use and had made a success of his immoral business. And these very qualities he now used to make a complete success of his reformation. He backed his purpose by the *whole* of his nature. And there is the next step in salvation.

If the question is asked how he was able to do this, there is, I think, a double answer to be made. Down deep, underneath all the acquired and evil habits of his life, there was the subconscious self, the deeper nature, trained in law and prophet, and love of righteousness—"forsomuch as he also is a son of Abraham." It was all there, buried, overlaid with the later and acquired habits, but not dead; ready to be called to life. And then that buried self in one swift moment was suddenly awakened at the summons of Jesus. "Awake, thou that sleepest, ... and Christ shall give thee light." It leaped to consciousness, threw off the burden of acquired sin, became alive and free. That is salvation. Jesus always appealed to the hidden self. He knew it was there. By the impact of his personality he supplied the needed springs of action. He both revealed the man that sin had made, and brought to life the essential man that sin had buried deep.

This is what may be called "the Soul's leap to God." The phrase is taken from a study of Browning by John H. Hutton, entitled *Guidance from Robert Browning in Matters of Faith*. In a chapter with this title he describes Browning's teaching of conversion, "his supreme message to our time." Hutton begins by telling of a new kind of bomb of which he has read which would explode at the touch of a ray of light. It would lie apparently inert and harmless until the light was turned on it. This would release its hidden forces. Just so, tremendous forces lie within the soul ready for escape to God. Jesus turns the pure light of God on one type of man after another, one with a small secret, another a more obstinate sinner, a third "loaded to the neck with the stuff of hell," until the hidden forces of the soul are reached and touched and the soul leaps up to God, out of any depths of shame and bondage, of cynicism and of unbelief, of commonplace and moral insignificance—"leaps right out of all of that to the breast of God."

The story ends with that immortal word of Jesus: "For the Son of man is come to seek and to save that which was lost." Not merely to save, but to seek. To seek and to save sums up the whole blessed ministry of Jesus. And the word "lost"[3] for him has its simple significance: Like a lost child, like people who have missed their way and do not know where they are. For all such lost souls, there is that same salvation that came into the house of Zacchaeus.

[3] Moffatt has suggested "dislocated" as giving the sense.

CHAPTER ELEVEN

SIMON THE PHARISEE

LUKE 7:36-50

A GREAT THEOLOGIAN REMARKED UPON THIS incident in the Holy Gospel, that it was more fit to be wept over than to be commented upon. And it is true. There is nothing more strangely tender in all the scenes that make up the perfect life of our Blessed Master. And this exquisitely beautiful story is a sort of simple drama—a drama of salvation. There are three characters. Simon is there, for he is the host. Jesus is there, for he is the invited guest. And then there is the strange, contrasting figure of the woman, the uninvited guest.

Simon was a Pharisee. To us the word has acquired an ugly meaning. It denotes a hypocrite. But in Jesus' day the Pharisee stood for all that was respected and respectable. He was the church man in good and regular standing. He was a well-known church official, a vestryman, a deacon, an elder. He was a high-class man known for his devotion to church and state. He gave generously of his income

200

to charity. He lived a clean, upright, God-fearing life. He was looked up to as a model citizen.

This man Simon invited Jesus to dine with him. Jesus had become something of a sensation. He had quite a following. Everyone was talking about what he said and what he did. And Simon wanted to have a close-in look at him. We can all understand that. He would invite him to dinner and see for himself what manner of man he was. Without doubt Simon felt that he was paying Jesus a distinguished compliment and felt that Jesus would be glad enough to find himself in such polite company.

And Jesus came and they sat down at dinner. And then the unexpected happened. Of course, in our Western houses, and with our Western customs, this never could have happened at all. But in the East the rooms are open to the stranger, who may pass in and out at will. And thus this woman entered and this dramatic scene occurred. The woman must have been notorious. Everyone seemed to know who she was. I suppose that they all stopped eating, and looked at Jesus. And I try to picture to myself how Jesus looked.

But we are thinking now of Simon. And if you and I had been there, is it not altogether probable

201

that we should have acted just as Simon did? If we can imagine such a thing happening in our house, would we not feel just as Simon felt? How else could you expect a respectable and responsible person to feel and act? If a woman of such a reputation should come into church and let herself down in our pew, and we knew who she was, and everybody else knew who and what she was, what would we think, and what would we do?[1] We cannot condemn Simon too hastily. It is a very disquieting story. As a host he quite naturally resented the intrusion of this woman, exactly and precisely as we would resent it under similar circumstances. Most of us not only would be shocked by the coming of the woman, but also would be surprised by Jesus' attitude. For he did not seem to resent it at all. There was no look of shocked surprise on his face. There was no instinctive withdrawal. He did not get up. Rather he sat quietly while the woman completed her strange oblation. But the others were quite naturally shocked. Her touch! Her kisses! Her hair!

Simon said nothing. Yet he had his ideas, which he seems to have been polite and controlled enough

[1] There are people in our churches "who would be equally shocked to see Christianity doubted or put into practice."—E. Stanley Jones, *The Christ of the Indian Road,* p. 119.

not to utter. See here, if this man were a prophet, if he had any powers of insight, any refined spiritual instincts, he would know at once what kind of a woman this is, and he would not be able to accept her attentions. Such was Simon's plain deduction. And the extraordinary and disquieting thing is that ecclesiastical respectability and religious conventionality would pass the same judgment today. Simon simply does represent average and actual Christianity today. I ask myself if the majority of modern Christians have gotten one whit beyond the feeling, the attitude, the judgment of Simon. Our conventional and typical Christianity is at least respectable, and the trouble is that it knows that it is. It has the conception of a certain code of honor, and of a certain consistency of life, which is well as far as it goes. What it lacks is imagination and vision and love—above all, a love that will take in the low and the depraved, the outcast and the despised, and look upon these with different eyes and judge them by different standards.

This story tells me that there is a gap, a gulf, between the mentality of Christ and the mentality of the ordinary Christian man and woman. I see myself and a whole company of similar-minded men and women represented in that room, "because Si-

mon represents just precisely and exactly that thing
which is so extraordinarily natural to us. He represents that sober and restrained outlook and attitude, tremendously self-satisfied, coldly reserved,
clean and hard, which passes its ruthless moral
judgments, just as Simon did."

I have called this a drama. Indeed it is—a tragedy.
But the tragedy lay not in the woman, but in the
man Simon. That indeed was the tragic thing. He
sat so close to Jesus, yet never once felt the beating
of the Master's heart, nor saw that his self-righteous
soul had more need of a Saviour than that poor
woman crouching at his feet. And that is the
tragedy today—of moral blindness. The real tragedy
of the world today is not that of ordinary sin. Our
very consistency, our very straightness, our very
goodness, within the limited meaning of that term,
blind us to the deeper needs of the soul. Simon and
Jesus sat side by side, but they were strangers to one
another. There lay the tragedy in this human
drama.

Let us go on with this story. Consider Jesus. He
had accepted the invitation of Simon, but there is
no indication that he felt flattered by it. His moral
stature, as we have seen, is revealed by his oblivious-
ness to social distinctions. When he sat down with

publicans and sinners and ate with them, it is not apparent that he felt as if he were demeaning himself. There is no sign of condescension. And when Simon invited him to dine with him, he does not seem to feel that any special honor had been shown him, nor is he awed at finding himself in the presence and company of these friends of Simon. One feels that he walks on a spiritual level above all of these lower divisions of class and caste.

We have here also another dramatic illustration of the irresistible attractiveness of the Person of Jesus. Consider the bold and unconventional thing which this woman did. It is not only that every natural instinct would have prompted her not to appear in public in this fashion. We get to the bottom of it only when we say that in Jesus what we call perfect goodness and perfect love were perfectly joined. For goodness in and by itself is not always attractive. There is, as we all know, a purity that freezes and repels; a goodness that is austere and uninviting. One of the deepest problems of the spiritual life is to make our goodness sweet and attractive, so that a person who knew himself to be a sinner would be drawn to us. When we have achieved that, we have reached the secret of personality and influence. And here is Jesus. We remember what he was—the whitest, purest soul that ever walked on earth, who hated and loathed sin in all its forms; "the highest, holiest manhood thou"—that at the least.

And she!—all her sad story summed up in one brief word. And yet she is there, in Simon's house, with every cold, critical eye leveled at her; and she is there for just one reason—for his sake. She had not come to ask a thing. She was there just for his sake, for him alone. His purity did not repel her. His goodness did not present an invisible barrier between him and her. Oh, there must be a defect somewhere in what we call our goodness. We are good, but we are not gracious. We speak the truth, but we do not speak it in love. We have virtues, but we lack insight and sympathy. Our religion has many things, but it lacks grace and charm. And it fails to do what Jesus did: it fails to love, to win, to draw. I sometimes think that one of the most tragic things in this world is the number of unlovely good people in it. One does not question for a moment the reality of their goodness. Yet the pity of it is, the more you know them the less you want to be with them, the less even you want to be like them. They have goodness, but they lack love. Dwight L. Moody once said a beautiful thing about

206

Henry Drummond: "Most of us make an occasional excursion into the thirteenth of First Corinthians, but Drummond lived there." That was the perpetual and permanent climate of Jesus' soul. And that is the secret of the attractiveness of Jesus. I have been reading *This Believing World,* by Lewis Browne. It would be difficult for anyone to describe the beginnings of Christianity in terms which are more at variance with my own ideas. Yet the author says frankly that there must have been a drawing power in the personality of Jesus quite beyond anything of which we have historical knowledge. I find a supreme illustration of that truth in this story.

We see another thing about Jesus. We see how he read Simon's thoughts. Jesus read him like an open book. He noted the cold glint in Simon's eye, the slight curve of his sensitive lip, the involuntary shrinking of his frame. Simon had not spoken—at least out loud. He spoke within himself. But Jesus answered as if he had been addressed: "Simon, I have somewhat to say unto thee." I have tried to picture the scene: the other guests, the silence, the bowing woman who hid her face—and Jesus and Simon as they turned toward each other. I have tried and I have failed. No, I cannot

207

picture that scene. And Simon said, "Master, say on." And I wonder, had he any hint of what was coming? Then followed the plain little parable of the two debtors, one of whom owed ten times as much as the other. And their creditor forgave them both. Which of the two loved the more? And Simon gave the only possible answer: the one who owed the more. And Jesus said, "Thou hast rightly judged." Then he went on and said something more to Simon. He said it gently. He did not raise his voice. There was no hint of resentment in what he said. But he said it just the same, and what he said must have gone home.

Simon probably imagined that Jesus was so much impressed at being guest at all, that he would not notice that the usual courtesies had been omitted. Now he was reminded of them: no water, no kiss of salutation, no ointment for the head heated by the sun, none of the things which a truly honored guest would have been sure to receive. Then Jesus pointed to the woman: "Seest thou this woman?" And for the first time Simon saw her with different eyes.

It was one of the most astonishing reversals conceivable. If Simon had been told that this man Jesus whom out of curiosity he had invited to his house would, before that meal was over, compare him unfavorably with a notorious woman like this, could he have believed it? Yet it had all taken place so gradually, so quietly, so inevitably. There were eternal issues and eternal judgments in the silence of that simple scene.

We come now to the third character in this extraordinary drama—to the woman herself. Gratitude had brought her there. She had seen Jesus, had listened to his wonderful words of life. She had felt herself shrived of her sin. God's own peace and pardon had entered her soul. And she felt a gratitude so profound, so all-controlling, that it caused her to lose all thought of herself, all consciousness of others, all natural timidity—that she might perform this simple, exquisite, eloquent service in her devotion to him.

The contrast between the motive of Simon, who out of intellectual curiosity and with a sense of patronage had invited Jesus to his house, and the motive of the woman in coming, is startling. They two were in truth pole-wide apart. And what we call salvation depends, it is here clearly revealed, on motive. It makes such a difference what that motive is. If, as in the case of Simon, it is a sort of intellectual interest, then that is one thing. But if as

with this woman, it is out of a sense of deepest gratitude, then that is another thing. The fact is, this
woman knew something about Jesus that Simon
from his motive would never know. And there are
humble souls in the world today who really know
more about Jesus than many wise men with all their
intellectual acumen and critical apparatus. Two
people were once talking about a mutual friend.
One of them said: "I met him the other day. What
an exceedingly interesting man he is." But the
other said: "Yes, you look at him that way. And I
do not look at him that way at all. I owe everything that I am or hope to be in this world or any
other to him alone." And there was a difference.
There was a mighty difference.

Remember, too, about this woman that she was
not a sinner when she came into Simon's house. If
we want to understand this story we must read: "and
behold, a woman in the city who had been a sinner."
But she was a sinner no longer. The miracle of
grace had already occurred. Indeed, that was why
she came. Otherwise she would never have come
at all. She was not the woman she had been. Her
soul was changed. All her life was changed. Because Jesus had washed her soul and made it clean,
she wanted to wash Jesus' feet. Because he had

poured on her soul the oil of gladness, she wished to anoint him with the most precious ointment she could find. Alabaster! An alabaster cruse of ointment. Yet even more precious—beyond the alabaster—there were her tears, and the hair of her head: symbols of the final, the exquisite, the utter devotion of a soul that felt its salvation; felt, too, that she owed it all to him. I think of what those tears were compounded. She wept over her past life. And I ask myself, has my life been so pure from evil, so freed from errors and mistakes, so filled with love for others, so empty of thought of self, that no blinding tears of what I might have been have ever dimmed my eyes? Tears of joy, of the sense of exaltation, of the poignant sweetness of the new life now beginning, of her moral self-recovery, dignity, freedom. So she wept at Jesus' feet. And tears of love for Him who had wrought all that. She anointed her King with her love, lavished upon him the tokens of her heart's devotion. What wealth was there, what treasure of contrition, of joy, of adoration! I have called this a drama of salvation, and so it is. For contrition, joy, adoration—these make up the characteristic elements of the Christian experience, which is essentially the experience of redemption. The essence of the Christian life is being in a personal relationship with a personal Saviour. And the sins of the head keep us away from such an experience more than the sins of the heart. Simon, with all of his respectability, was a stranger to the experience into which this poor woman had now entered.

For see the end of it. See the contrast between what Jesus had said to Simon about himself and what he now said to him about the woman: "Wherefore I say unto thee, her sins, which are many, are forgiven; for she loved much." And to the woman herself, to whom he turned in tenderness: "Thy sins are forgiven."

> She knelt and wept and with her untressed hair
>   She wiped the feet she was so blessed to touch.
> And He wiped off the soiling of despair
>   From her sweet soul, because she loved so much.

And she passes out of our sight, but she passes also into the bright light of the glory, the life of God.

I said this was a tragedy. I said also that the tragedy was not of the woman. We come to the tragedy now. What was the effect of all of this on Simon? What did this mean to him? "And they that sat at meat with him began to say within themselves, Who is this that forgiveth sins also?" Still reasoning, still puzzling, still discussing, still arguing. And Jesus there. And the miracle of salvation before their very eyes, when the same story, the same miracle might have happened to them. And the hour passed, the occasion was over, and for them it did not happen at all. "And he said to the woman"—and not to Simon—"Thy faith hath saved thee; go in peace."

So Jesus dealt with Simon, so also with the woman. So also, if we be Christian, will we deal with those of whom this woman is the immortal symbol. "Perfect love, we say, is not to be expected. Yet Christianity is either perfect love or it ceases to be Christian. Christianity has not been tried and found wanting; it has been found difficult and left untried. Nevertheless, to read the Gospels in church, to pray for love, to preach about love, making not one single effort of love in our dealings with the abandoned or lost—is not this manifestly to live our lives outside of the Kingdom of God" [2]

Thus Jesus dealt with men. With what insight, wisdom, sympathy, love he met and solved the spiritual problems presented to him by varied types of men. The world is filled today with people just

[2] E. Stanley Jones.

like them, who look for illumination, freedom, the gift of inward power. To be the helper of one's fellow men is perhaps the greatest mission which anyone can perform. To share in the Spirit of Jesus alone equips one for this highest of all tasks. Thus, our deepest prayer will be that he may be found in us, that, like him, we, too, may be among the healers and helpers of mankind.